*Collected Poems 1955–1975*

D1394232

By Peter Levi

POETRY
Collected Poems 1955-1975   *1976*
Five Ages   *1978*
Private Ground   *1981*
The Echoing Green   *1983*

TRANSLATIONS
Yevtushenko: Selected Poems   *1962*
Pausanias: Guide to Greece   *1971*
The Psalms   *1976*
Pavlopoulos: The Cellar   *1977*
Marko the Prince *(with Anne Pennington)*   *1983*

FICTION
The Head in the Soup   *1979*

PROSE
The Light Garden of the Angel King   *1973*
The English Bible   *1974*
The Noise Made by Poems   *1977*
The Hill of Kronos   *1980*
Atlas of the Greek World   *1980*
The Flutes of Autumn   *1983*

Peter Levi

# Collected Poems
# 1955-1975

Anvil Press Poetry

First published in 1976
New edition published in 1984
by Anvil Press Poetry
69 King George Street London SE10 8PX

ISBN 0 85646 134 2 hardback
ISBN 0 85646 135 0 paperback

This book has been published
with financial assistance from
The Arts Council of Great Britain

Printed and bound in England
by The Camelot Press Ltd
Southampton

ACKNOWLEDGEMENTS

For permission to reprint *The Gravel Ponds* (1960) and *Water, Rock and Sand* (1962) to Andre Deutsch Ltd; for *The Shearwaters* (1965) to Clive Allison; for *Fresh Water, Sea Water* (1966) to Black Raven Press. Other collections were published by Anvil Press Poetry.

'Good Friday Sermon 1973' was broadcast by the BBC on Good Friday, 1973, and subsequently printed in *The Tablet*. 'Canticum' first appeared in the *Critical Quarterly*.

*In younger times I joyed in the sun's ray
and wept at nightfall, now in my sunset
daylight begins in doubtfulness, and yet
holy and tranquil is the end of day.*

HÖLDERLIN

# Note

A book of collected poems before one is dead calls for a short excuse. This collection includes every book or pamphlet of poems I have made public, and a number of new poems. Several of the pamphlets in particular were obscurely published, and a high proportion of what I have written is now out of print. The circulation of all poetry is limited, but to limit the circulation of one's own poems even further would be gratuitous. I have not revised or selected those poems that have already been published, so I am not able to claim that these poems, only these poems, and all these poems are what I would like to be remembered by. But they do represent at least half of a lifetime's work. If a poet wants to be believed, not to be applauded, he must inevitably wish to present the whole corpus of his writings.

I have made one verbal change in the poem on the art of satire, as I have made changes previously in that poem, where time had bent the point of an example.

P. L.
*Easter 1975*


It seems odd to have left out the obvious. These poems are intended to give pleasure, though since they were written at different times of life the pleasures intended were different, and some poems express grief or a despairing courage. But I do not really think that Life is a Platform; when I named that collection I was more interested in Death being a Pulpit.* Life must be what it can.

P. L.
*June 1984*


\* ¡ Pupitre, sí, toda la vida; púlpito
   también, toda la muerte !
         – César Vallejo

# Contents

# 1    The Gravel Ponds

A tightening net
traps all creatures
even the wildest.

Too late
the young cry out,
and the innocent,
who were not wild enough.

Bodies and tears
are useless;
so few years
are helpless;
free creatures are never wild enough.

The noose closes
making the tragic
young the pathetic
in slum clearance houses.

Never, O never in the long distraction
of the heart's inaction,
never will a cry shake
that prison, or wildness wake.

The young were like those swans
which with folded wings
swim on the gravel ponds
on late June evenings:
like doomed stage characters,
pursued murderers
or slum lovers.

**2**

Saecular decay can be
arrested only in agony.
Triumphal corrupted stone
hangs down from the mind's bone,
air- and water-hanging trees
eroded images
weep that time must be
repaid in mental agony.

Father's death, swell of the moon,
glitter of a shrinking one,
night orbing home her food,
chemistry of suffering blood,
or the young heart or the old
stiffening through degrees of cold
in the mind can only be
drops of an elemental agony.

Atoms of the refracting brain
should in one mind one grief contain,
wars in a tear, whole systems in a grain,
and in the mind alone,
the suffering eye of noon,
the element and the agony might be one.

# 3

The Catalonian Communist
is dead, or abroad, or doing fine,
with a wife to keep him warm
or an exile magazine.
and the heart's fog-horn, dull in mist,
can bring no living ship to harm.

And those are out of sight or dead
whose bodies bore the terrible rain,
or who in knots of nervous wire
revolved the images of pain,
who when they lived, the slow heart fed
each hungry nerve with streams of fire.

The rough wind smoulders in the skies
trailing new-coloured dews of ashes,
heroic murder's out of fashion,
the uneasy cities burn in flashes,
and death, the general lover, cries
from under street level his passion.

And God and I and Communists
with little intervals of farce
play glove-puppets with schoolmasters
and terrorize the working-class:
the dead with suddenly sweating wrists
cry out for birth. No birth occurs.

**4**

An angel sat on a tomb-stone top. He sang
a country song.
The wind is in the pine tree, shepherd,
that hums so pleasantly: and your flute is pleasant
the angel said. Shepherds talk in the shade,
a half-remembered story, how a nymph
loved Daphnis, and he died in a crowd
of mortals and immortals, and the lions
howled for him in the hills, and lurking bears
dropped hot tears for him. Sing you shepherds
said the angel, Sing when thin cicadas
chir in the heat, and the thickets have their leaves.
Autumn is coming that will pick them clean.
Winter is coming with his claws of ice
to break the flute and bend the pleasant pine.
At the year's end stands Christ in a pillar of fire.


**5   On a Theme of Samuel Palmer**


We went along in absolute silence:
it was coming on to dusk of a clear
hot day, there was a harvest smell.
Armfuls of red apples blushed in the shade,
leaves wound in and out enjoying the cool.
Chestnuts were dying. It was the day of the dead.

Inside the woods there was a cave,
and a wise woman as old as a Sibyl
weaving her hands in the glowing air.
She stood three hours under the blossoming tree
bloody with fruit, may trees in flower,
bloody with fruit, loud with prophecy.

# 6   Fragments of Colour and Light

Confident and young
in superb alleys
the great chrysanthemums
hold up unruffled
faces of petals,
and startle the eye
with their possession,
and lend the whole light their quality:
the whole light equally
hovers around these reds
possessed by
these few, these flowering heads.

So all night time
once in Byzantium
among flickering stems
in a tulip garden
served the purposes
of the hundred candles
on the backs of tortoises
who slept or trundled.

Amazed night
belonged to them,
backs gilded bright,
between stem and stem.

# 7    Elements

The ewe's hot body weighted his shoulders,
the road splashed up dust.
If the sun,
he thought,
if one
of these days the sun—
    wailing of a song and the clang
    of a bell of iron—
he sweated as he humped the ewe along.
If one
of the children of the sun
were to come,
turn the sun
to a yellow chrysanthemum,—
(hot on his neck
and straight back
the ewe drowsed)—
    flowers of paper
    floating in the light—
the strong
man trudged on
carrying the sheep.
If the sun fell,
he thought,
drooped on its stalk
with a dying smell,
or if a flower
of burning paper . . .

# 8    L'Aurore Grelottante

Three counties blacken and vanish,
rivers run unlighted and silent,
lamp by lamp of the city came, went,
into the utter dark, which was my wish.

In my scarred thought this city
burns to a ruin under the visiting air,
among the ashes of whose luxury
the young barbarians shake their scented hair.

Bitterer, deeper, in my desolate thought,
a lonely and a self-murdering love,
uninhabitable ashes, every dove
murdered, every winged buzzard caught.

The wind rises. At this time of night
condemned men lie quiet on their beds.
Birds start. Vagueness clears to light.
The wakeful old can let fall their heads.

The wind rises. A workman coughs in the cold.
It rises. Volleys and lines of mist
push from river to river and find no hold.
Leaves fall. Blood runs cold in the wrist.

## 9

By currents or by that slow wind
who drops his equal favours on all seas,
among these hardly moving waves carried
I sailed to Sicily and the the shores of Aetna.
Without fear or passion,
but reading the intelligible and clear
movements of stars, and without
abandonment to the shifting influences.

I came to Sicily and to the shores of Aetna.
It was as if
some god in the remote, bottomless sea
long since had twanged his horn,
and with his many and his silent steps
pursued, pursued,
among uncoupled furies.

The mountain dropping fire,
death by fire in a twisting
unbreakable net of fumes,
so that I ran down sweating, terrified
out of the ghastly caves and from the just
furies.

No reason now to hide these tears.
I pray I may be carried
far off in the triumph of some god
among those islands such as at sunset show
their pure and austere line.
I pray I may be carried
away from this place,
away from these stars' magnetism.

## 10   H. S. L.

So hard to think
we could have come
to a formal stone.
All autumn
any boy at ploughing
must have seen
its lonely station.
Better at night
the first visit:
when weeping millions
of stars or stones
smother personal fright.
Estranging half-light
was better for this visit.
A monument must stand
for the pain of remembrance,
it can contain
a complete passion,
just as a heart the entire
pity and terror
of body and of air.
No time or place
here for my service,
but this: *Vale in nomine trinitatis.*

## II

In midwinter a wood was
where the sand-coloured deer ran
through quietness.
It was a marvellous thing
to see those deer running.

Softer than ashes
snow lay all winter where they ran,
and in the wood a holly tree was.
God, it was a marvellous thing
to see the deer running.

Between lime trunks grey or green
branch-headed stags went by
silently trotting.
A holly tree dark and crimson
sprouted at the wood's centre, thick and high
without a whisper, no other berry so fine.

Outside the wood was black midwinter,
over the downs that reared so solemn
wind rushed in gales, and strong here
wrapped around wood and holly fire
(where deer among the close limes ran)
with a storming circle of its thunder.
Under the trees it was a marvellous thing
to see the deer running.

## 12

He met her
at the Green Horse
by the Surrey Docks;
Saturday
was the colour of his socks.

So they loved,
but loving
made nothing better—
drowning cats
in an ocean of water.

What more,
what more could there be,
days or nights?
Nothing
to hear or see but dances and sights.

So they loved,
like the aimless air
or like walking
past shut doors
in a never quiet street and talking.


## 13

The fox-coloured pheasant enjoyed his peace,
there were no labourers in the wheat,
dogs were stretched out at ease,
the empty road echoed my feet.

It was the time for owls' voices,
trees were dripping dark like rain,
and sheep made night-time noises
as I went down the hill lane.

In the streets of the still town
I met a man in the lamplight,
he stood in the alley that led down
to the harbour and the sea out of sight.

Who do you want? he asked me,
Who are you looking for in this place?
The houses echoed us emptily
and the lamp shone on his face.

Does your girl live here?
(There were no girls or sailors about.)
I have no girl anywhere,
I want a ship putting out.

He stood under the lamplight
and I stepped up close to him,
his eyes burned like fires at night
and the lamp seemed dim.

He came closer up and pressed
his crooked knee to my knee,
and his chest to my chest,
and held my shoulders and wrestled with me.

It was the middle time of night
with five hours to run till day,
but the sky was crimson and bright
before he stood out of my way.

I ran past as quick as I could
and the wet stones rang loudly
along the wharf where the ships stood
and the sea lifting proudly.

And age can be a time
to make a hedge or a rhyme,
cock an eye at the morning,
for blood and heat to resign
their passionate storming.

Then let a fall of snow
mute time's overflow,
let blood's courage and heat
be chill and run slow
with an austere beat.

No passions can save
an old head from the grave:
each blood-controlling moon
that drags wave after wave
dims and hurries down.

Old age can be a time
for a garden, a rhyme,
some solitude of mind,
for the flute and the bell chime
and music of every kind.

A vain ironic mood
keeps it cleanest and good,
since only irony
can keep the truth in the blood
from a mere motion and liquidity.

## 15

Teach a hawk to come home to the hand,
eyes to be hooded, whipping wing quiet,
the ambitious senses and mind understand
only by conquest. Persist; let

your courage assault his will, your pride
match the bird: ambitious intelligence
needs to know him, call and make him glide
out of the air, within reach of sense.

Teach a hawk your hand: you'll have him
obedient on a wing-tip: in flight free
but known, but mastered in each limb.
A mastered hawk has no disloyalty.

Other wings your power can't master:
we have seen swans in a pair on the wing
through a gloomy evening black as disaster,
defeating sense and understanding.

Sometimes unmastered wings our hearing fill:
we hear them thunder and sweep, plummet and dive,
and in an Arabian wilderness there are still
birds never seen by anyone alive,

birds that without stooping to the hand win
passionate knowledge, peaceful desire:
in whose image we sometimes imagine
this whole world is a phoenix on fire.

## 16    In Memoriam C. W.

He was a small, delightful, active man,
I was glad it was on Good Friday he died,
no one surely since the world began
had died so old and so innocent eyed.

Just as a frost in late autumn blights
some apple out of reach, withered and red,
and it seems the worst loss of those bad nights,
so it seemed when we heard he was dead.

All that suffering and age
were not so hard to understand,
but death in his ultimate lion rage
striking the cross out of the old man's hand—

and many a frost burns them in the grave,
old men's bodies worn to pure bone:
yet as if death were mocked somehow and could have
nothing in his hand but a skeleton,

or as if some spirit blew from the mouth like breath
and blood chills and pales, and bone sags,
or as if that tempestuous lion death
could be pacified with a few old bones and rags.

## 17

The lads of course arrived too late,
but still, for a small fee
—Christ being already crucified—
they chopped down the tree.

## 18    Stars

Out of shaking
air and time we came,
at a touching taking
godlike flame,
or like that bird which owns no mate or pair
but hangs for ever in the astounded air.

## 19

When poisoned Socrates,
blinded, with stiffening knees,
died and grew cold,
it was the young were with him, not the old.

Young passionate Plato heard
and honoured every word,
mastered his mind,
knew what he knew, was blind where he was blind.

His mind with a strong wing
hawk-hovering, questioning,
thought it no rest
to build in fabulous truth his tree-top nest.

Plato mapped the air,
what winds were foul, what fair,
at last grew fat,
fluttered his feathers on this wind and that.

He nested in dark trees,
forests of mysteries,
took playful flight
in skies ambiguously day or night.

With the old it's always so,
their fancies come and go,
attract, repel,
with death in sight and life, heaven and hell.

It was with irony
that old man claimed to see
his godlike One;
mystics, and not believers, claim the sun.

There was one scorned to be wise,
grew old with sober eyes,
drank with profound
religion poison, while the young stood round.

**20**

What if the world were a horrible mad fit,
human reason sand, and God a mere unknown,
and no philosophies could temper it
to shivering flesh and nerve, breakable bone,
but the mind's vigour alone?

I would not choose to be masked in any defence
beyond the fight and heat of an animal,
and heart's power against heart's pretence;
some wild thing's ways, not copied or learnt at all,
some quiet of innocence.

**21   Alcaics**

*inter silvas Academi . . .*

No, there was no one. Torpor and loneliness
put them to sleep, dead each in his bird-loud tomb,
   quietly caught into lapse of motion,
     whom the impersonal woods lamented.

We, too, have seen them, crooked and water-eyed,
holy, the old—rain strung from the loaded air—
   the terrible old with their coughs and wisdom,
     under the trees in the truth and darkness.

If there were one voice only I hoped to hear,
one falcon mind whose stoop in his solitude
   simply to see would be truth and goodness,
     here I have haunted and here lamented.

## 22

My mind reads whether in a flight of magpies
or in a dusk wind or an owl's feather
always the myth of the gardener,
and beasts gentle in his gentle eyes.

I think of Adam's lions at the stir
of any sleeping beast—as hounds follow scent,
of running creatures, and of his punishment,
and his deer, moving without cover.

We are nowhere free from this disenchantment,
there are always stories and fantasies
bred in the bone, compelling us to this;
and any chance note seems a faun's lament,

the iris in late flower and the clematis
wear their colours like a dead fashion,
groves seem receding vistas painted on
the plaster walls of desolate palaces.

Nothingness can never so appal
the heart or chaos recognized distress
the mind as such heavy sadness,
like hanging clouds too thunderous to fall.

But now the myth turns, leaves caress
the light, cocks in the farms are crowing,
and diamond-clear skies are echoing
green praises with a grave redness.

Now every lion seems a crowned king,
and weedy rivers and the sun's face
seem the repaired images of grace;
for Adam's son, winds and finches sing.

Like a giant the myth runs its race:
no gardener but Adam's son could appease
these human archetypes and images,
which no one's heart could bury or mind displace.

It was as if the world's boundaries
were suddenly flung down, or as if skies
grew clear suddenly in the sun's eyes,
and time stood still, out-towering centuries.

## 23    Digenes Akritas

*vos exemplaria Graeca/nocturna versate manu* . . .

That hero was strong,
outlaw and captain:
but shaggy Charon
forced his body down
wrestling with him.
Streaming blood, he despised his fears,
and the ghost of Plato sang in his ears.

But he was wise too
in his mind, he was one who
committed his passion, master, to you,
the simply good and true,
knew proved in his own body what he knew.
The mind's courage exists in isolation,
committed reason is a hard passion.

Mortal passion
is felt in common,
reducing men like the action
of lust in any whore's conception.
When blood ran in a river down his chest,
Plato's wise ghost understood the test.

In three days it was over,
and that black wrestler
had forced him lower with a heavy shoulder.
He died, lonely huntsman and gardener,
clear-tongued, taking the Sacrament with tears.
And still Plato's ghost sang in his ears.


## 24


He walked by rivers in that strange half-hour
when swans on the darkening water drift,
and drakes flighting in the obscure air
seem to know of a dark that would never lift.
He often wandered there.

I have heard him speak on some unsolved question
as if his mind's discovered unity
were to pursue pure dark with a clear reason
moving in a prophecy of mortality
from season on to season.

And yet it was always some trick of light
in a bare, wet wood, or it was some dim
pastoral hillside quickest drew his sight,
and bareness more than ruin moved him,
or any tree at night.

## 25

The innocent seeds of light drop in the eyes
and generate prophetic images,
the visions of the harmonious and the wise.

I meditate the mysteries of design
on a formal urn shaped in porcelain
whose neck has a multitude of petals or flames,
or bars of colour, not fitting the names
of paint, and certainly no natural scene,
a red and blue and green and half-green.
On the urn's body a turning
dragon claws the air and seems to spring
with a chiming roar of his powers,
twisted, in a falling dust of flowers.
I often trace the line of his belly and tail
and yet the dragon and the flowers seem pale
to the blue and the red in simple gravity,
and green, and half-green—or to be
dissolved almost to sheer mobility.

Just so when I look in the obscure
but prescient and still crystal sphere,
I trace the immortal self-consuming bush,
and every laurel tree burning to ash.
Reading this grave, simple sign,
I meditate the mysteries of design.

## 26

Over the roof, high in among the gloom
you come to a remote, airy room,
a hexagon resting on pure light,
where mind can shoot to any height
or in a ripe curve down the leaden dome
dissolve in mere formality
of that grave, simple century
that here for a mind at peace hung this home.

And any daw constructs his branchy nest
among blue air on trees never at rest,
and hangs and floats as if the infinite sea
were an element of liberty,
or swims above some bending woods, content
to be imprisoned in any motion
of tree, air, bottomless ocean,
swaying with thoughts the entire element.

How soon the mind returns to such a place
where loneliness and mere extent of space
summon, receive and hold it motionless,
and how these circling thoughts confess
long traffic in such godlike liberty,
in never fathomed deeps of sight,
and uncontracted bounds of light:
how used the mind is to that mystery.

All afternoon vague shadows
cross and recross the floor, clarity grows:
all afternoon on a stir of breeze
daws dawdle around the trees;
evening drops them chattering, drowsy night
quiets them, and utter sleep
rocks the woods, and black and deep
air opens all around to the waking sight.

We pass the night's hours, that pleasant time,
breathing peaceful winds, rocked by a chime,
drugged with dreams, or else with dark or a bright
melting moon-ring or mere star-light:
or else awake sing to help time pass
until smoke hangs and wine's confused
and then a bottle's broken. Time, abused,
hurries off dawnwards from the crashing glass.

Also night and morning
we solemnise a Christ-like act asking
for mercy, and still the circling mind
not knowing what it willed to find
returns to this symbolic room, and ends
by charting with a devoted sight
whatever roof juts up in the light,
and mumbling over its memories of dead friends.

No thought of the mind was ever out of time,
no science and no knowledge and no rhyme
ever climbed further from that leaden dome
than this six-sided room,
and here my mind returns, day and night,
accepting with an instinctive ease
this nest where the mind hangs at peace,
this intellectual liberty and light.

## 27

A dust of birds
blowing in the east,
the shaggy sun creeping like a beast
homeward—these seem the authentic words
of desolation.
Yet high up, beating air
with wide wings, a pair
of flighting geese in a lonely exultation.
Making north they go
with a powerful mind,
making for blind
dark and sea-pools where the salt airs blow.
Geese going over: high
in a trailing mist,
wingbeat, twist
of cloud, darkening sky.
So the flying reason
seeking its ancient places
moves scarcely seen among chases
of cloud, chimeras of this bitter season.

You could say it was like that pear tree
with wads of buds just opening,
and innocent of any calamity.
The shepherd of Hermas might be piping,
and other symbols. It would always be spring.

Or if you wanted, you might say
it was like an eikon, something Byzantine
or early English where in some way
that frightening happiness of the divine
mind had drawn his face with a burning line.

Or say it was the first and the precious tree,
and on its wood blood-breasted robins sing,
in the office of whose humanity
the friendly shepherd trusts. Prefiguring
death. It would always be autumn, never spring.


**29**


In a corner of Eden
the one-horned black
rare rhinoceros slept in the shade,
water among the reeds softly swam
yellow and green the ripening melons hang
softly slept.
In the hot light once
he went, stinking shade drops
dark over his head,
in Eden once
easy-bellied he lay
and breathed a gentle breath such as yellow
fruit or any sleeping beast may.

## 30

I reverence John Cotman and John Crome,
Sandby and Cozens. You are my masters, Richard
Wilson and David Cox, but long and hard
schooling of your thoughts you give me.
And one died famous and mature, and one
in London unhappy in half-light,
whose world was discomposed, or who never
came into port in his coloured Americas;
yet dying, and his eyes crowded with sleep,
with a divine mind, as once in his summer,
drew Norfolk wind that herded the flooded woods.
I reverence John Cotman and John Crome,
and will with green honours hang their heads,
whose thoughtful schooling is my thought's best part.

## 31

I owe this winter some sacrifice,
more than bemused night's gentle breath,
some rite of the blood's heat, some honour of death,
to enchaining February some better price
than this spring-musical wreath.

As hounds cry after the hare and the fox
and fill shaken woods with bell music,
so I in my blood cry and seek
as ice-packed Dnieper shouting among his rocks
his slaughter of ships and cocks.

Five o'clock ploughs its morning furrows
yellow over a farm,
trees wade in mist, echoing strangers
wake to the cock's alarm,
shivering day comes new from the same cold
that buried the old.

Beautiful monsters asleep on the ocean floor
stir about to hear
the remote clamour of the quayside and of ships, half-heard
in a water-muted ear.
The antique girls serenade empty seas
in sensuous voices.

High up some rocky place like a waterfall
one breathing cypress tree
sways and splashes fifty clear feet
from its light extremity
down into shadow. It seemed the ideal station
for a hermit's meditation.

Up there a wild old man lives with the moon;
a cock crows in his mind,
his eyes are like a beautiful sea-monster's,
quiet, wild, blind,
but still his age like a haunted waterfall
rings with call after call.

## 33

Like strangers who casually press
under a silent dome
for a minute's idleness,
I into death have come
and into stillness.

The friend of man
Epicurus knew this:
there are no riches.
Long ago the wind ran
among the rarest trees,
tore pear and lemon down
and rare-headed irises.

The peace that was his choice
beats and rings with noise,
what frost and wind spare
and the rainy air
some fairground methodist will blast with his voice.

Time, wind and thunder have no home
but their own darkness,
and I in my own element have come
to stillness.

**34**

If I could be
the explorer of my own liberty
by knowledge and possession
    as settlers understand
    their small island
with a devoted and entire passion,

it might seem to be
some forest isle in some fabulous sea
of which I only dream,
    oblique, never possessed,
    not wind-distressed,
not visited, fortunate, so it might seem:

as if liberty
were casual and could never be
a deliberate, perpetual possession,
    as if the mere flight
    and undiscovered island were the delight,
and not the explorer's or the settler's passion.

My liberty
is an island and a continent to me,
and no nuance of grace or any passion
    ever dare I neglect
    which might subject
its not yet charted bounds to my possession.

# 35    Longwall Street

At eleven in the morning in a full street
an enormous haycart went by
with a mixed smell of freshness and heat,
and scattered a wisp or two, used and dry;

which in its lumbering progress
dwarfed and over-rumbled everything:
it left a heavy smell, and a small mess
of scraps of hay, settled or drifting.

So on some swell of the year's tide
and ripening into serviceable death
orchards expect a half-descried
October with his coarse and autumn breath.

And at other, at sharper times,
the long bodies of the carted trees
bundled like a strange peal of chimes,
or half-alive, half-murdered images.

## 36

Immense façade. Heavy grace. Decay.
Hot tireless air. Greatly planned
fine-coloured stone, proportions blotted away.
Carved cornice shuddering into sand.

Monkeys fight and chatter. Trees grow
where once were steps in the sun, press
close to the walls. Green and yellow
dissolve in flickering wells of darkness.

A night-jar cries or sings
celebrating a rite half-understood:
dove and pelican fold prophetic wings
calling loudly among the flowering wood.

## 37

Under my feet where I was sitting
I could see the skin of the water darken and flash,
and in and out of the darkness a bat flitting;
under the bridge was as cold and dark as ash.
In such water scarcely visible
willow branches tangled together seem
to grow both the real and the unreal
from a single tree, or any reflected star
to burn like a scarcely bearable
drowning angel that can never (being so far)
be rescued, never (so bright) be at peace,
never climb dry, never sink lower,
but lost, hung on the air's inconstancies.

That white mare flicked up her heels as nimble as ninepence,
when she was young. But now she never stirs more
than from one leg onto the other, old mare. She'll die
but she was a lovely creature. That ragged dog
went mad in spring with the smell of so many rabbits,
and had to be shot, poor dog. Oh but they all
die, all grow old, the snorting gryphon and the tiger
in the young woods, the untamable salamander,
and the gentle beast, the dear white unicorn—
who was buried in a meadow in Calvados, and the birds
come to sing to him there, but never will wake him, lulled
in his meadow of poppies. But Mrs Hanratty wept,
and said it was a lovely creature. A lovely creature, she said.



**39**


A Buddha on a leaf cannot eclipse
my mind's mechanical apocalypse.

Angels and pit-ponies are blind,
stark necessity rages in the mind.

There blood is and dust, atom and star,
but in that dark no quiet planets are.

The fragments of a Christ's face
shatter apart to mere space;

Oh but his nature and name are written there
in Chinese circles of black atmosphere.

**40**    *for Gregory Corso*

I

In a brick city one pastoral evening
truth and I walk home.
The electric night shuddered.
The sun stank of gin
(and she asking him in).
To me neither proficient
in truth nor in poetry
this street and moment seemed to be
landscape, territory,
the significant illusion
dogging my nature home to black confusion.


2

In the street between nine and ten
two shabbily dressed Jamaican men
were walking.
The river breeze
crept by touching their faces.
Shadows guttering. Livid light
licked them walking.
The melted feet of Christ
stood or streamed inch-deep
and touched, devoured the people in the street.

Light, melting from the pages of the books,
light devouring libraries,
light burning the cornice of an eighteenth-century chapel,
light dissolving birds into bright air,
light dissolving itself into darkness,
black light streaming from the bodies of dissolving sailors and
   running in clear streams,
the landscape, clay and limestone and volcanic rock, nothing
   but black light.
Self-murdered from the beginning of the world.


## 41  Alcaic

Out in the deep wood, silence and darkness fall,
down through the wet leaves comes the October mist;
  no sound, but only a blackbird scolding,
    making the mist and the darkness listen.

## 42    Hymn

*for seven alto voices,*
*from a school play, 'Orpheus' Head'*


Harsh face among the pure planets,
whose constellated influence
drops deeply, deeply drops, drops
in a bright essence,
whom night never forgets, never forgets:

Broken star, head of dead Orpheus,
distorted voice of distances
cry sleeping, sleeping cry, cry
in the wild spaces
which sleep never visits, never visits.

Harsh voice among the pure planets
whose music-making intellect
drops deeply, deeply drops, drops
from a sheer abstract
which night never forgets, never forgets:

Broken star, head of dead Orpheus,
whose sacred head alone can speak,
cry sleeping, sleeping cry, cry
in a wild music
which sleep never visits, never visits.

**43** *for Francis Wyndham*

Though I should have to walk
whole winters by this lake
where swans without a sound
but like unruffled images are drowned,

or where a late sun hangs
from his transparent wings,
should work like a chemist
among the faint leaves and corrosive mist,

yet I can strain and hope
for words and for a shape
which unregarded might
praise reason and be bare or clear as light.


## 44    Proposals for a Poetic Revolution

I can praise no one but the simply wise and good,
whose words like savage conches haunt and ring
in an echoing daimonic solitude
of the suffering and dead.

They fear no horrors worse than what has been,
but purge the images of their age and passion
as if into ridges of a pure and thin green
receding into rain.

And I can praise no mythical creatures,
breast-heavy Pomona or running Faunus,
no innocent monsters with half-human features:
only reason and nature.

But if when God envisioned Adam
some moonlight man with weeping iron scythe
cut down those dreams of corn and of reason,
I praise this swathe and grain.


**45**    *to my friends, for Julian*


Tonight the big winds are rising,
whose breath will disturb this whole remote
valley, and make the wires ring
high up and down the scale with a hollow note.

Septembral trees sweep their dark masses
across and across, now a river's voice
bellows from far off, now woods release
shrieks of death-longing into a riot of noise.

And even in so quiet a place
winter comes; whose antique face tonight
hangs close, troubles my sleepy ease,
broods among rain and ponderous storm-light.

One turns over an old newspaper,
its yellowing grim rumours of violence,
the slow degrees of murder; I should prefer,
supposing neither capable of defence,

black private water, a leap into suicide,
where hours and seasons ritually move
in a public dark no violent wish can divide
dull-chiming leaden feet from grave to grave.

But that you, my hopeful friends, live on,
each one in his own hermitage or room,
thinking of weed the winter sea bangs down
on a stone beach, sad aftermath of storm.

Now that the paler west
is fainting into rest,
and landscape disappears
I recollect with tears
thoughts which sometimes sleep
but rot like guardians deep
in mental scenery:
by whose tenacity
contemplative I see
in a wood or a landscape
one rigorous grace of shape.

There were some whose first journey
touched undiscovered country,
put roots into new land,
and some who understand
rivers, shapes, tones,
a country's bones,
all at a mere sight;
could smell trees at night,
moved in crowds of birds,
fitted mountains to words.
Others had leafy tents
for a wandering innocence,
or thought themselves paid
by sadness or shade.

Some in a valley or wood
courted solitude,
among whose wild cover
comes no shepherd or lover;
whose voices grew to be
hollow sonority
and resonant gravity.

One sees a reflected face
in the architecture of place,
makes music of natural noise,
pure colour, personal voice.

I recollect with tears
thoughts as sharp as fears,
my landscape half disappears.
No shepherds sing in its arms,
its trees scatter no charms,
its lines are sober and bare,
fine-drawn on lighted air.

## 47    Elegy for Richard Selig

*Part one (October)*

Neglected Eldoradoes of the mind
have no resonance that matches
reverberating death: nothing moves
under his snow of ashes.

And ragged crowns of cloud do less
to circumscribe that head
than any plucked, fresh-looking leafiness,
to death appropriated.

No loss of a friend
can be contained
in an agony of mind,
no mind's patience
outdoes the images of its feared pretence:
but that the peregrine truth, hooded in the heart,
will sometimes start
into clear height, and stoop, stoop on sense.

*Part two (December)*

Summer's exact coin
is now new melted,
and winter half gone.
The faceless sun
rising in a sky of sharp grey
infuses hanging vapour with a clear
lemon wrack of light,
gets big and grave, and trails away
into pale writing in the obscure air.
Not so cold as the hand,
Not so vague as the heart.

In midwinter I can easily recall
the coldness of the rooms,
every leaf slanting to its fall,
the coldness of the water,
trees stark naked, Thames running,
the coldness and the weight of the water.
But not so terrible as the rooms,
Not so echoless as dead laughter.

I can recall how still
three leaves were
that seemed to hang on air,
among thin trees round an abandoned quarry,
how still the black water
how still and silent there
reflecting a guttering sun, caught in the trees' hair.
But it had no depth of coldness like the hand,
no shivering like the heart.

*Part three (May)*

*'Of true Falcons gentle an Eiry is never found . . .'*
(Notes to the POLY OLBION)

The distance and the landscape break
into a chasm of mere height,
and infinite in regressions take
new colour from the intenser light,
in whose untamed unweeded lake
the falcon screams and spires awake.

The sun's young image glitters bright
among the foliage of pale trees,
the falcon like an anchorite
hovers among bright images,
and foliage, black and green as night,
slaked with the sun obscures my sight.

That hovering bird which no one sees
observes over the continent
the infinite lightless distances
in which this tilting world is pent,
dead choirs of planets drift and freeze
among the orbits of his ease.

And marking the slow moon's ascent
he claps his lightning-flashing wings,
his eye is lonely and innocent,
for him the cosmic system sings,
in circles of a wild content
at rest in his own element.

*Part four*

Now the moon-crusted earth
evaporates to a new birth,
and long invisible falcons spire
higher than air in light and fire.
Stranded here I scribble a name
where nothing lives but praise and shame,
and nervous wire and sculpted bone
tense to a tuneful skeleton:
till no wish remains at all,
but that we should be musical.


**48**     *for Denis Bethell*


He stood frost-white and nerved with fire,
his terrible eyes seemed drowned or dreamed,
in which his crystal-breasted sire
alone was recognized and named.

His voice was like the antique breath
shaken from an age-yellowing shroud,
or bare as the wind on a fell-heath,
clanging like water, and as loud.

He moved moth-lonely among the press
of shadow-roofed, close-rooted trees,
which tangled into a black darkness
their casual perplexities;

and high rock valleys knew of him
where hawks on broad wings wheel and hang,
at his hoof-beat stillness of dim
mountain clouds listened and rang.

And often in his solitude
too near the intensely deepening skies
he had heard some deep hound-haunted wood
shaken into music of cries.

But beyond cry of hounds or men
in the heat of his natural courage
he had run, and no one has spoken
of the agonies of his grief or age.

And how can I speak of his death?
who died in pain, hunted, yet
the harsh whisper of his dying breath
seemed an ultimate symbol of quiet.

It was that first bare moment of morning,
the pale and glorious sun half risen
out of his world of mist, woods ringing
with long calls of the birds, thoughtless of men;

end to end a long valley
to the sharp horn sounded and echoed,
the voices of hounds howling free
roared, but the huntsman in silence rode.

I can say nothing of that huntsman
but that the ground trembled beneath
the beating of his hooves, and rang
like distant iron: and his name was DEATH.

It was that terrible moment of morning
when at rest among his blue invisible peaks
the running sun seems almost to cling
on empty air, then sheer downward strikes.

And many woods had heard their strange cry,
and water stilled as voices of the dead,
and gradual lifts of open fields and sky
had marked for pity hunters and hunted.

Death cried on his hounds, far on
over a world of bare pasture and thorn
ran as he ran, and always when they were gone
hill and wall echoed the atonal horn.

Time ran headlong, and the sun fell,
trees groped for light in stock-still attitudes,
and cold and deep and ageless as a well
the sky died over the noisy woods.

In that black depth of trees Death took him,
horn silent, a few hounds howling alone,
terrors gone, the corpse stiffening, grim,
as if a mourner might come; but there was none.

## 49    Poem of Place

Oh, it was certainly wild weather,
any memory of cloud-break seemed a painted one
in the presence of those howls of thunder
seeming to hang and to echo so long.

The rain was very beautiful,
drifting as hazily as a smell
across and across slopes where the full
river threw its voice as loud as a bell.

A few withered leaves were guttering,
not yet quite rotted away,
so grave and still they seemed to cling
to the long expectation of such a day:

which now cradled the whole thin wood in
its hanging valley, its mind too strange to reach;
near here children in a damp ruin
play among words, and the dead teach.

## 50    Elegy for Lord Byron

Prospero bored with any romantic gesture
knew there was nothing left but to die:
and Ariel, innocent and simple creature,
far out of sight of his wise and powerful eye

survived in each delighted element
but never spoke or sang again,
(having lived in intellectual discontent
and nervous horror of all living men).

What else maddened Empedocles? What moved
poor Gray so to phrase his native gravity?
but the artist's wish to have loved and have been loved
in a landscaped distance where no love can be.

(And what can I say to diminish this,
except to report strange flowers, noises of birds,
drawn in restrained perspective, whose life is
in the incorruptible artifice of these words?)

In every cry of the lamenting mind
from every imagined sanctuary each one could
once in the past have placated, they ran blind
into the long perspectives of the receding wood.

And neither love now nor religion
protect sad Ariel set free,
and no words can do more than beckon on
cold Prospero, dying unhappily.

How should we live at the worst then?
Like aimless music (is there anything more sad?)
Like comic characters who seem to be men;
be natural, be gentle, not be mad.

Or dressed in the antique patches
play pedant, captain, harlequin,
in scenes whose atonal formalities
outwear your rubbery bounce, my conscious grin.

There exist no other authentic
heroes, however remote
(except perhaps that mere music
seems to exist) in any other coat.

A sleeping Buddha occupies my mind,
and half-obscures its whole religion
by mere presence, contemplative and blind,
the intolerable comedy goes on.

Italian Harlequin was a Christian,
and yet his savage comedy went on,
and the God in whom this thought began
is Christ, in my imagination.

Think of an architect of sad music,
or of the Rake howling in Bedlam,
whose mad and lonely mind moved tragic
into that quiet which no act can damn.

## 52    Humanism

I pray to those who released
such storms in the mind and the world
as no one else in our time
can ever harness, but most
to those who endured those storms.

And I shall stand with these
on the smashed ancestral glass
which hung in its frenzy of heat
above our coldness and peace,
with a bare acceptance of light.

But I pray most to those
whose act of suffering
claims no tears or praise
but is voluntary and strong
in a long triumph of peace.

## 53   Future

If ghosts existed there are some men
who could never effectually belong
to a thin as air congregation,
who'd find the trailing end of some bitter
wind's or yew-tree's slanting thunder
(weeping or not) their place to shelter under.

If ghosts exist I shall be one of them,
knowing with love each individual bright
station of any heavenly spirit;
yet never approaching high for long,
but as if the refracted alleys of distance
were the reality of my thin substance.

No one will need to fear contact
with spirits as content as we shall be,
the devoted private friends of humanity;
we being ghosts shall long ago have swallowed
our private lie, our secret disgrace,
and winnowed mind to influences of place.

I have no words or song for the brave
but to some bitter eye may have
some photographs and aphorisms,
which Blake-like hang above black chasms,
clapping their iron-riveted wings,
for whom the cosmic system sings.

Not for those great by blood who endure
all inhuman discomfiture
cheeks flushed by mental discipline,
but who in rage seen and unseen
by spiritual choice or chance
like spirits in mid-air can dance,
to whom most deaths and histories
are despairing generosities.

Not who in politics or an ascent
of mountains grapple discontent,
but who preserve green-pickled grief
in nervous tics of unbelief,
not who by mental visions redeemed
whip passionately the nightmare tamed,
but who enduring in silence
their solitary ambience
choose light without dark or pretence,
the revolted and the repenting sense,
since human virtue is that end
which hopeless bone and mind intend.

## 55    Political Poem

A dandelion's head erect
howls in the tortured intellect,
a cloud can murder men and press
whole armies into feebleness,
the smell of hyacinth drunk in
is the revolution's origin.

Two crickets creaking in the grass
can freeze the continental mass,
one vixen round her litter curled
can freeze to death an age of the world,
zoo goats on an artificial crag
are the revolutionary flag.

And the fierce puma and the hot ape
pull their own entrails out of shape,
and the young lovers whose sun
is an absolutely perfect one
deliver over seas and lands
to the violent dead with bloody hands.

## 56    For Christmas 1958

In mid-December this huge building
settling to grey composes its sad colours,
its cliff-like hulk, perpendicular force,
into a sleep as gentle as a moth's wing.

Here islanded away from the sun
in an extreme of distance, a few boys
cold in the wind learn from no one
the comic melancholies of a brass voice.

Here I, poor flotsam Christian,
perceiving only the angle of a lead roof
against a designed stone, must write as I can
what I can neither imagine nor speak of.

My mind as if in a stone prison
waits for the young gaolers and the wise,
fearing always violence, dissolution,
the island exiles with wind-haunted eyes.

And no harmonic or tempestuous rage
can exorcize from those fierce eyes the wild
terror, but this painful and grave image:
the sadly loving woman and the child.

## 57    Style

I have no myth to express this passion,
which knocks the skull, shaking down words.
Which houses nothing but its myth or passion,
not capable of words or of emotion.
And anyway, in time it had to happen,
I can no longer understand for whom
it seemed a possibility of death to be
young, or a multitude of flowers or questions:
each one a myth, a language and a passion.
I have one myth, and an outworn emotion,
not capable of its true language or passion,
or of my true language, of this passion.


## 58    For Poets in Prison without Trial

All day teaching in some classroom
I can hear your maddened pens,
scratch, scratch, where human foreknowledge comes home,
O images of violence,

O condemned poets, O dead who write
with iron pens in your unresonant cells,
and into mere blackness of the wasting night
drift out like solemn cries of ruined walls,

O dying poets in your terrible rooms,
breathe out your useless messages, your fact
to the inconsequential gaoler when he comes,
the inevitable beauty, passionate and abstract,

and O if some confusion of daylight
drops in the end like leaves on your faces,
then make your eyes star-purple, planet-bright,
like natural forces, echoless voices.

## 59    Themes

Ship-building emperors commanded
these night-obscuring giant beams,
with open-work like ribs defended
what is from what merely seems,
among those timbers old
the young sea-captains sailed.

Storms of a classical illusion
broke open, bit by bit, the mind
in oceans where a bleak confusion
on a ruined shore has left behind
dead Plato, litter of broken wood,
redefining moral good.

Some broken stone, sublimely quiet
poses against an open sky,
(the subject populations riot,
the discipline of the troops is high),
now in the officers' mess
they mention happiness.

And young men in romantic places
curbing an adolescent rage
reform the lines of their cold faces
in a dead father's still image,
whose mental life is now
this service which they owe:

by a nervous trick of rhetoricians,
judgement, language for events,
to deny all images, all visions,
to choose gay-coloured ornaments,
self-mirroring man and woman
in a lost image as human.

But when these mental forces break
no natural anguish can uncover
the lost ship in the draining lake
which a savage hermit brooded over,
who is now defined again
in a quiet craze of pain;

and those first virtuous professions
haunt angels and their whispering throats,
while the sad wise in grave processions
(deep-coloured gems, light-coloured coats)
let fall their heavy tears
gaunt music for lost ears.


## 60     Portrait

This mind keener than sense
had drowned its innocence
well-deep in a mineral
recognition of death,
had taught its wing to brush
as a half-existent moth
might on mere moonlight
as if it were a wall
where no water could call,
and yet which of us all
could drop or hang so deep
from so quiet a flight?

## 61 Evening

Oh it was a peaceful sight
where the sky had caught its edge,
that transparent yellow light,
(trees stood tiny on the ridge)
quarries lapsing into night,
bare rigidity and height.

So contemplative and blind
I can turn my head away
carrying with a fearful mind
such crepuscular mental joy
as (being like no other kind)
seems innocent and undesigned.


## 62 Letter to a Pupil, for Leonard

You, smoking on a cold platform at night,
remembering the languages of schoolmasters
will count among them this unpitying verse,
this harsh-eyed landscape and this boring light,

which then, like mute machinery breaking up,
shall discompose to iron-dark fragments,
to bleak words, violet dark, discontents,
the unfinished typescript and the unpolished cup:

and vapour like some memory or damp ghost
will smother your vague eyes in train-echoing night,
in valleys spiked with blue and unnamed white,
or the sea's surface, or the sea almost.

I imagine you remembering some trick
or half-silence, some half-inadequate wish,
or half-hearing some voice of the outlandish
curlew's fastidious music

which never forgets or submits,
but always calling fills this whole savage
landscape with his life and natural rage,
like angels' cries in visions of hermits.

Or else settling deeper into your coat
you raise from the dead some blind Socratic bust
and sniff its smell of wisdom and of dust
letting the prose-style gurgle in your throat:

like one who can recall now nothing
but a once heard, long meditated cry
which leaves the bare round of the echoless sky
in all its elements broken and ringing.

And stranded there with a few late travellers
you will from meditation understand
the nervous laughter and the shivering hand,
proverbial sayings, mental disasters.

**63**   *for Alasdair Clayre*

The book I read this morning tells you how
to become a heron in the world of the dead;
I should prefer (it came into my head)
cheerfully shitting robin on his bough

his ripening colour and his tireless throat
to those great flap-wings and solemnity:
you have to walk Novembers through to see
the personal life expressed in his sweet note.

What I want in the world of the dead is leisure,
dying dissolve my numinous discontents
into a place, the gods into elements,
where time, water and air conspire to pleasure.

Things used for pleasure humanize all places,
green vacuous city, castle and riverbank,
the evening bars, station and taxi-rank
inscribe humanity on uninnocent faces,

and lovers walking in the freshening light
let fly and wander their untroubled sense
in an intensity of innocence
—time, air and water, shadow and night.

Or later when the drifting moon surprises
moonlight walkers, the nothing they pursue,
the river-mist, the fields exhaling dew,
where shivering birds sing as the sun rises.

Nothing but human use can glorify
field, mist, air or light,
common possession and the common right,
and the need of growing which the young live by.

In the world of the dead if there were one
I can do without the violet and the rose:
the democratic young are my heroes,
the casual voices, air, rain, sun.

## 64 Placation

In gardens cultivated too long
huge monkey-puzzles and boughy cedars breathe:
while in the fountained pools of shadow underneath
an underwater gong

clangs and quivers with an endless beat,
and mingling undulations move among
these coarse-haired August images, silent now too long,
and now the intenser heat

in one revolving prism of topaz light
(one father and consumer of images)
explores the receding wings of ruined sceneries,
and gently dims to night:

yet at a touch of flame or evening breath
the yellow topaz flushes into pink,
and beast or garden spirit or bird come down to drink
their pool of dusk and death.

## 65   Thoughts out of Doors

There was a scarlet liquid sunset
incinerating half despaired of hopes
in smoky dusk, and that it seemed so wet,
the boy scouts were carrying coils of ropes
splashing with stiff hands up mud-sodden slopes,
clatter of rooks, blue shadows such as grow
thickest in woods, and then the rain also.

This freedom from ancient absurdity
gave new foothold for functional intellect,
like solid climbable air which the eye was free
either to contemplate or to select,
to conjure it into mind, but chose direct
eyesight of woods, unable to relate
those bare tree-tops to an ecstatic state.

And then that it was wet underfoot,
the usual hill looked misty and distant,
we were talking, someone had a wet boot,
I can remember thinking how want
is never in common, because instant,
private usage of common languages.
The rain drew round in slack intensities.

**66**    *for my mother*

Husky Regulus made of lead
hangs statuesque over his pond,
the crimson nenuphars cluster around,
tortured Regulus never moves his head.

But past the thin lines of the nearer trees
the ground goes rolling in a miles-long trance
of seen but never trodden distance
up to a high-backed hill, stretching at ease.

And both of us now or in past time
remember a day of such pure clarity,
this glistening light that never seems to die,
but hangs for ever dissolving in a lime-

green of half-yellow evening sky,
until the new-mown fields and hedges seem
to be peaceful decorations in some dream,
confusing shape to a blurred intensity;

for instance that day which grand and cold
so hardened into dusk a year ago,
—we sat not noticing it at your window,
curdling the pale downs with transparent gold;

or just as now some long shadows advance
or railway darkness wakes us travelling
in landscapes where a cold bird singing
fills with his voice the echoing distance.

## 67    Portrait of a Schoolmaster

And I should wish to draw you, caught so
head on one side, hand on the tea-table,
that nervous posture and those bright eyes able
to relax in accuracy at a window,

in a view of hills reclined distantly,
olive-coloured and tall, or like clear
Latin speech, weighed and fine in the ear,
designed by ice, or tortuous irony;

or else exhaling aphorisms like brittle
fire of a nineteenth-century rocket,
—by fascination seeming to forget
what this lights up so briefly and so little:

the mildewed landscape which no mind can cure,
hypocrisy of the heart's incompetence,
all the sad images of violence
and decorous religions of failure.

Watching a withered dawn soon blown away,
the emerging hilltops and the cock's alarm,
his mind in hard islands ringed round by storm
searched among temples whose noise was the sea:
—there the sun fell so equable and calm
his eyes picked music out of solitude.

And one fine morning in a stunted wood
he might have quite brushed off this wasteful dawn,
and in the unvaporous classic light have seen
those pastures which his mind like wind pursued,
his proper landscape, one not glimpsed or drawn,
but populous harbours and the exact rock.

Poor mental traveller where else could he look
for that bleak marble and salt-roughening green?
Not in the jumble of this country town,
strip-cultivated streets whose patterns lock
the relaxed lines of meadows terribly in,
enclosing life from soils not colonized.

There at a thought some shepherd's gunshot eased
severe folds of the cold-wrinkled mountain,
he could land there friendly from his daydream
on the mere beach itself where a few pleased
fishermen slept or children hemmed him in
by the cafés with his notebooks and his sleeping-bag.

**69**   *for Dom Moraes*

We took no notes of contemplated light
    or of delight
though (each one writing in his room alone)
    we could have done,

we were confused from treason by the exact
    spark of a fact,
touch of a self by salt and bone surrounded
    or self-compounded,

each one by love and season friend or fool
    of the beautiful,
wrote personal poems read by everyone,
    naming no one.

**70**   **Images of Departure**

Before the sun came out
there was a misty sea,
waiting on the jetty
I thought, If a whale should spout.

A single pink line
marked east in the sky,
not enough to judge by
if it would rain or shine.

The sea was quite placid,
I watched a porpoise track,
black spokes on a grey back
convulsively lifted.

And small shearwaters skimmed
with a harsh, comforting sound
as if they echoed round
from a mountain not climbed.


**71**    *for Christopher Logue*

Blue irises when I was a child
playing in a profuse garden
gauzy and big on necks of solid green
showed daily faces neither fresh nor wild
but gently unobservant where I played,
and water squirted in a thin cascade.

But I could never wish to return
to childish time or to that garden sound,
praying often over the wasted ground
while minutes real as thistles tick and burn,
for physical justice, metallic chime
of industry which is the end of time.

I think often impotently of it,
but my best thoughts and words are too often
such irises as fibrously glisten,
like a dead moth's reanimated spirit
drinking alone in vegetative ease
watched by a moss-encrusted Socrates.

Perhaps it was never the flowers,
their sharp colour and aimless patterns
which austere time by so long labour earns,
but only the wages of gardeners,
among whom like a working man he stands
and moves between beds with his steady hands.

**For Julian Going to America**

When you arrive in so sad a city
whose strong fingers teach the sun his place,
chant hymns under your breath to liberty,
her amazing stature and her blank face,

reflecting an abstract rage for her honour
in an unreceptive hand, petrific eyes,
(so I, self-prisoned in my resonant hour
set free these lines as music of her cries).

Now to the groaning of murdered Europe close
your ears: they only can condemn
who breathe an indifferent air's brightness, and those
who are not the first person of a poem:

not in hotels, forewarned by horoscopes,
softly treading the intolerable maze,
but lost from arguments and mocked with hopes,
and unprotected by their lovers' ways;

(so I among these wet woods writing
or in this high room on a wind-rocked night
half-vanish into the clear glass of learning,
the dead boy into crisp yellow and white).

Oh fear for yourself in that city,
for the poet's first person and his pride,
waiting at dusk or later maybe,
throat muffled, hat pulled on one side,

for the eye's confusion and the phoney dream,
the bedside telephone, the waking mist,
the city autumns offering what they seem,
his tears, his sleep, and love his diarist.

As I below bare Longridge stuck with pines
cower from violence, meditate disgrace,
the atrocious echoes and the long designs
of this stiff portrait, my unloving face.

Since love like freedom shows a ruined front,
a tenement house whose windows peer out blind,
distracted from its perfect self by want
of the fatal lover and the reflective mind.

No poet, no free man or lover
who lodges in that distant city
can walk safe by imaginary power
where its death is, or where its ash will be.

## 73     The Garden in Early November

In crazy garden-walks this endless season
flowers and reflowers the bushes,
breaking as if by reason
into light lilacs and hanging roses:

and I shall miss them, walking between
frosty beds in the winter,
masking turnings in fresh and pleasant green
or tiring out seasons like a gardener,

thinking what grows now in my mind,
nothing with a root or leaf there,
no tree, no root buried or blind,
but my cracked head lets light in everywhere.

Some atom of clarity then, or sparkling seed
breaking open, shining, overtopping
boughs that scrape heaven in phototropic greed?
Not that. Not greenery. Not anything.

## 74    Meditation among Woods

In this place meditating always
in a few woods between iron ridges
whose vigorous growth like untaught images
can ornamentally chill and give delight,
I can no longer praise
though stellified the exotic travellers.
Considering winter walks of schoolmasters
on afternoons part misty and part bright,
—the bronze violence of the shadows
among the unanswering fells and cold hollows—
I praise redemption bought,
days scorching the damp in their long flight.
Rain falls, rivers sprinkle a long noise,
some tiny gaieties of birds and of boys
which populate this houseless hillside,
recall what Christ suffered and his martyrs taught.


## 75    *for Anthony*

All day I draw conclusions from the sky
ending in politics and tears and sleep,
stroking rough grass and choosing for worship
green lizards or the religious butterfly,

which in today's sun flutters his peacock wings
or else dusk-shaded, folded out of sight,
becomes some paper-thin tissue of night,
whose liberty is the clouded wind's howling,

and shapes of hilltops which have piled up here
by ice and weight, the imagination's bone,
drop shadowed flanks which seem as smooth as stone,
or sprays of light hung muted in water;

76

and gashed with streams these slopes have crevices
full of thin trees and smelling of garlic,
where light-mouthed water throws a voice so weak
it eats away whole hillsides quite at ease.

I occupy my head with this small noise,
being one whose ironic unhumorous ways
speaking in water and in rock should praise
these stiff hills' face, and their indifferent voice.


## 76    Roman History

*. . . such and more strange*
*Black night brought forth in secret: Sulla's ghost*
*Was seen to walk, singing sad oracles . . .*
                                        (Marlowe's *Lucan*)


I am one whom such intense lights surprise,
I have no words for the azurous fragments
and dews of stars moving with lighted eyes,
whose bodies burn from such black nourishments.

Running among nebulae or pursued
by the unnatural voices of comets,
in shadows measuring the moon's magnitude,
or what sea in what rocky channel frets

by the reliefless crags so overstepped
among them darkness ponders in a ring,
I clean my eyes on colours which have crept
on twists of a sea-shell, or the resounding

galleries of a dry stone city,
this self with its apparitions and its fatal tones,
there meet winter, disturber of the land and sea,
and Arcturus who rises in a shower of hailstones.

77

## 77 The Greenhouse in October

Relaxing among hanging plants
I notice a cold light which slants
in through the panes from brittle air
(gardens are places for despair)
putting a butterfly to sleep,
textures rough, colours deep,
and trails of leaf transmute their height
through falls more fugitive than flight,
vague-fingered things: yet out of these
I take my words and my wishes.

Rain-threaded, gull-wheeling, bell-clamorous air,
by wind shifted, by smoke lightly weighted,
in which sirens beautifully despair,
no monument crumbles uncelebrated,

one incandescent, vaporous element
diffusely fingering the bare troughs of seas,
shifting at the sun's rise and his descent
in swirls of fog in the brown estuaries,

rain-bitten air, whose bass whispers reach
elaborately through the wooded silence, lift
your voices like the syllables of human speech
which is man's gentlest and most perfect gift:

cold air which in the earthly paradise
combed leaf by leaf from the sharp-scented wood,
touching the ribs of Adam into ice
breathing him sleep deathlike in solitude,

girdle the grimy ribs of this city,
let bell, rain and gull which inhabit
stone and steel fingers groping so high
sound in the street to those who live in it,

and mortal features moved by heavenly grace
as natural Adam turned his head sleeping
let it look upward with a human face
gull-haunted, rained on, bell voice carrying,

and cross-channelled by the twelve voices of wind
and dressed in mist as Adam when he woke:
stood for a moment as if he had been blind,
and bent suddenly over Eve, and spoke.

## 79    New Weather

It was the new weather last night,
releasing grass washing away mist
colouring the whole sky with bluish light,
or some ice-cold reflective artist

who in a year-long self-analysis
or celebrating the moon's obscure birth
might have struck on his true music which is
the easily running light and standing earth:

I celebrate new weather with new words,
counting the pigeons in the snow-cold air,
listening to small voices of the other birds,
walking in the wind that sweeps this poem bare.


## 80    *for Peter Hacker*

These quiet autumns hide despair
old rhetoric, my mental state,
day after day through misty air
the dry echoes reverberate.
Now climber on his cliff, too scared to climb,
I search from rock to rock, misted in time.

Gardens and roads when I was three
first lured my wandering sense to spin
these crystals of maturity
to expose imagination in.
Winter brought dusk, autumn released in rain
the dropping leafage with its dying stain.

Then in the pages of school-books
I found stories about my life;
the masters gave me curious looks,
I fiddled with a small pen-knife;
all savage pleasures, and that pain and shame
vanished in moon and mist when autumn came.

The antique writers, the dead style,
horrific symbols, bleak comments
seemed altered in a little while
to a nervous kind of ornaments,
or roughened shells or craggy rock faces
worn into shape by cold autumnal seas.

All those philosophies have gone,
since pleasure, doubt, the sense of death
teach schoolmasters their own lesson
in voices tangible as breath,
and adolescents, studying what I write,
note the dead foliage and the dying light.

Now an intense reflective rage
by seasonal rebirth and loss
rips away words, page after page,
ringing eros on thanatos;
I study bare landscape, question the dead,
listen to cold rain falling in my head.

Romantic hermit, smoker, letter-writer,
whose meditations move too long among
the imaginary winter sound of the sea:
here entertain calamity
its impetus or terrible apparatus
to suffer or to speak
by the breakwaters on the unnerving beach.

Predatory hungers of the herring-gull
that raucous sea-bird occupy you now,
concerned by nothing human, while the long
blasts of the ocean wind still speak among
those tall headlands and foreshores where you wander,
so avid for some cobalt gleam of the sky
or the wet sand's shining obliquity.

Southward from here your shabby classic garden,
colours and hanging smells under a hedge,
two broken statues and an unkempt tree
decayed into maturity,
mid-morning shadows and a sliding question,
animal sensation of a mind
scoring like music, seasonal and blind.

But shy salt-tasting contemplation hangs
on the cliff-face above the resounding shore,
where the surf shrivels and the green sea swells
in glittering levels;
consider such places with their easy tang of endurance,
that water, rock and sand,
eyes stung by wind, and salt powdering your hair and your hand.

It was nearly dusk when we began to climb,
we passed through a deserted garden
between a few bushes, where now and then
some bird called out his echo of softened time.

We passed under a long, kept alley
where branchy trees guarded us like a dream,
outside a dead house by a musing stream,
water subdued whose origin might be

far up on the unfriendly hillside,
some powerful cistern no engine can take,
or jangling dribbles out of a black lake
making hollows of evening seem less wide.

A wooden bridge humped in a broken shape
between two slopes of lawn that seemed designed
by a long departed gardener in whose mind
neglect had overwhelmed his small landscape.

We walked on in file, following
a path so silent and so overgrown
it seemed this whole island like quiet stone
hung in its sea as a hawk hangs on the wing

quite level in a late ray of the sun,
and no motion could touch or trouble it:
it was some thought the flighting mind had hit
or lost imagination landed on,

and yet this garden and the few late birds
which still uttered were visible and clear,
not such as under lights of dreams appear
but hard in the eye and mind, netted in words.

There was a garden fence and then the wet
ground and a miasmal haze of damp,
I stopped to try the long beam of my lamp
and feel the candle-end in my pocket.

We were moving in open country
between two knolls towards a rough hillside,
in dusk not deep enough for a guide;
the hot sky seemed an endless clarity.

But now the stone peak of the mountain
was out of sight, hidden among ridges
which stooped above us, and whose shelter is
crag-headed Halleval's abrupt curtain.

We climbed out onto the open hill,
where always among mosses and the impure
hill grass the red deer pasture
between these grave mountains moving at will.

And now the hill had opened like showers
suddenly concentrating in heavier rain,
as if the divinity of this rough terrain
were grasping by half-knowledge what was hers,

and flung her wide arms out, making the crest
fall in a slope of yellow or of blue,
and made it lie as gradual and true
as that long line which streaks the fainting west.

It was that light falling which half defers
its suicide in the sun's own paleness,
it was those gilded beams which can distress
lost eyes moving in autumn flowers.

There was no smooth pallor or fantasy,
but the direct and dying sun, outright
shadow perspectives etched in fields of light
from an airy ridge, remote simplicity.

And further now below, foliage of woods
still broke and darkened in luxurious seas
where the tall hills like mental images
upreared their never speaking solitudes.

And always as we climbed we strained to hear
(but too far off and now not visibly)
fierce intonations of the self-echoing sea,
austere voices of the shallow water.

The sun had gone and it was colder now,
a late bird or two went overhead,
the immense half hillside seemed to name its dead
shaking down silence from its level brow.

We climbed into the track of a small stream
which spoke and clattered between stone and stone,
then out along the bank of another one
whose force and coruscating falls might seem

the exact and powerful images of some mind,
existing in its own wilderness here,
whose untrained voice inspirited the austere
boulders and pools where it cascaded blind,

so loudly it dashed this sleek and foaming
white hair of mountain water down;
the rock was like a cold and echoing crown,
where as we climbed we heard this water ring.

Harshly as human intellect it fell
in a cross-grained perpetual music
which thread from thread no hearing can unpick
or unconfuse that atonal cry and bell.

We climbed high up, from fall to fall
the water sounded in an endless chime,
someone talking from time to time,
or a dropped stone, or else no noise at all.

It was as if some painter in his age
could concentrate painting to a few bare lines,
stark colour of the romantic disciplines
annihilating thought to a quiet rage,

in which he worked in an earthly dusk and light
shadowing deep the immense intractable shape
of the entire tall-valleyed landscape
by equations of colour and of night.

We came out at last into a place
where yellowish grass gloomed in a level
floor among ridges like a lightless shell
not far above us darkening into space.

But high beyond them, over a round shoulder,
stone of a great peak had caught the moon;
we moved across towards it, and soon
we were cut off from the noise of the water.

Its face of rock curved out into the night,
it rose out of a gradual litter
high into darkness till what seemed so near
vanished in black, remote and out of sight.

And now the bright moon newly risen
was floating free behind the peak,
painting the waves with glittering music
in bare rock bays whose tides had half fallen.

High up behind its peak the moon floated
making the wind seem solemn and slow,
but we were caught in hollows of shadow.
This mountain was as silent as the dead.

And in strange touches of a reflected light
the topmost of the rough grass on the entire
motionless circle shone with sudden fire
and we through light moved onward over it.

It was here we came on sand and rock,
and bent to the wind picked a laborious way
between the cracked off monoliths which lay
here and there on the slope as if to mock

tall Halleval with a broken strength,
or as if some glacial ice had carried them
like frozen blossom broken off at a stem
trailing down fragments from its endless length,

as long ago this toppling stone leant
low-headed under the scarcely moving ice,
and drifted snow could speak its long service,
and chanting wind was never silent.

But now far off and in a wilder sea
where floating cliffs swing and fret
that landscape which we imagine and forget
in storm and mist hides its sterility.

And always under that soft-handed sky
beyond the pack-ice and the barrier mist
hover snow hawks which never stoop to the wrist,
and blue-eyed shags and Wilson's petrels fly.

Between the enormous boulders we found
a place to rest out of the wind,
the last shelter before they scattered and thinned
to a jumble of fragments on the uneven ground.

Overhead the sky spread its fine
impenetrable moonlit blackness,
and Halleval visible less and less
bulked upward vanishing into a darkening line.

No hermit could ever have chosen
the speaking wind of that desolate place,
but it moved undisturbed on the broken face,
making the whole night seem open.

There were no voices or music in it,
no choirs of ruinous echoes which practise
long songs in their disconsolate paradise,
and no presence of any spirit.

But the mountain was windy and bare,
and we were crouched scarcely speaking,
a flung pebble struck with a quiet ring,
there were no birds in the whole empty air.

So there for a long hour we waited
as if by mental visions we had done
with the day's heat and iron-burning sun
here first received among the invisible dead.

We waited for that hour of night which dumb
instinct of a god or beast prefers
guiding far off the tireless shearwaters
which in obscurest night will sometimes come

to fill the whole dark with their wings and cries
penetrating these cliffs with a broken call,
and suddenly settle, populating all
the northward faces, so thick out of the skies

not even spray or mist can drop so,
or crowds of appearing stars or flying lights
from burnt forests on wind-tormented nights,
or settling foliage, or blowing snow.

In moonless dark they fly in
among the stone breeding-places, glide
out of a mist from the whole mountainside
shaking the black air with a mocking din,

crying in high voices
suddenly broken off, and scarcely seen
in nervous arcs of flight; whose cries have been
heard far off from here among quiet seas

or off storm-circled islands where they fly
in fives and threes low over the water
forward and back one way and the other
articulating that unearthly cry.

Then on a night of utter darkness
these things of nerves return to their birthplace,
and high on Halleval's north-pointing face
in hours of mist, cloudy and windless,

the shearwaters settle among these stones,
and the young birds come out of their hiding,
safe in the gloom, hearing the whole fog ring
with swift wingbeat and flight and crying tones.

We crouched waiting for the wind to die
or the bright moon to sink into a cloud,
but the savage wind still bellowed as loud,
and the remote moon trailed its clear glory.

And all that night the moon shone
while we in the shadow of the breeding-slopes
wandered and murmured, nursing our hopes,
and the heavy-bodied wind bellowed on.

Between dusk-coloured rocks like a ruin
in the place where the mountain was most bare
there was a sudden whirring in the air
and the first shearwaters came in.

Crying they swung as quickly down as if
to split the wind to a structure of levels
or a surdic intricacy of open cells,
calling and rushing until the cliff

murmured their thin cries and soft wingbeats,
and threading through blown air like a surface
they wove that massive dark with an alien grace
which never dies or pauses or repeats.

We moved in pairs across the mountainside
and here and there some cranny of weather or age
or some pale lichen or green saxifrage
flourished a moment in lamplight and died.

And now and then as quiet as breath
one shearwater flighted down to the ground
between long beams of light flickering round
in allegories of surprise or death,

or else a sudden light held him
rocks echoed suddenly with noise
and lifted by a tiny crowd of boys
he was fearlessly blinking his dim

eyes confused in the torchlight,
silently fingered marvellous thing
he seemed too weak or light for ringing
then whistled and vanished in receptive night.

And still over the heads of the searchers
the wind was full of weightless whistling cries
and (passing too swiftly for surprise)
the uncanny wingbeat of the shearwaters.

Among blasts of the wind they slid at ease
or nervous in the moon's brightness
could flight far into the brilliant dark and press
deep among those obscure intensities;

where night received them flying.
But we on the wind-desolated cliff,
coats buttoned, fingers going stiff,
still wandered calling and answering.

We climbed up higher, pausing to speak
or moving uncertainly or two by two
drifting upward as kites above children do
high into dark beneath the invisible peak.

The entire surface of his level brow
hangs broken in crags and hollows
each one in forty-foot high shadows
beckoning who comes up, as we came now.

There was some saxifrage or stiff grass
under my hand, between rock and rock,
the mad wind was crowing like a cock,
the sky was cold and black transparent glass.

Out of sight the flighting shearwaters
uttered their disdain or lament,
distant voices came and went,
we climbed high up among the tall boulders.

The still rocks lay like a quiet husk
of the world burnt out and forgotten
before the first man's savage garden
drenching their hollow sides in windless dusk.

And then the level tops of rocks were skinned
and darkness peeled easily away
in a light like a remote mental day
and the full fury of the imperious wind.

There was a light so bare and equal
falling on that hard surface
it seemed some breathing element of the place
or infinite transparent fire let fall

from far above the white-eyed moon,
some bodily but penetrable darkness
strong with interior light, such as can dress
in dazzling azure at the point of noon

or in some desolate drift of colour or cloud
which hangs dissolving in the vaporous west,
autumnal glitter, presentiment of unrest,
the winter sun's self-knowledge and his shroud.

But here this placid light hung and shone
through the whole dark from mountain to mountain,
glittered among valleys as fine as rain,
dropped steady on crest and cape of stone.

Big Trolleval and Arkeval seemed near,
the remote moon was walking on the sea
paving the waves with bright transparency
terrible as justice, nervous as fear.

Space seemed alight, it was as if
the enormous wind had in his clumsy dance
quite brushed away the night's thin substance
dropping it broken round some distant cliff.

Far out to sea absolutely nothing
moved but the wasted water,
mile beyond mile there was no shelter,
mountain beyond mountain, nothing.

Light and time outnumbering sense
fell in a complete quiet,
as if this sailing moon could never set,
or time were intellect and providence.

Then down again from the massive wind we crept,
half-mastering stiff legs and drowsy sight,
slope below slope, moon-shadows and night,
and in the hearing of a stream we slept.

*Stonyhurst, Isle of Rhum*

## 83

*et non erit in te odor ignis*


In the morning the pier railings are wet,
The boys high-dive into the autumn sea
like salt-washing a deep stain of the sun.
Humanity deserts the public beach.
Humanity should have died out in us,
we should be as the stones are, should retire,
retire, retire. New creatures be walking
hand in hand along the edge of the tide.
It could be colder. Tomorrow's children
will couple on the rampart of the cliffs.
My generation is humanity.
The season in the air burning and bright.
I am in love with these few gulls and birds
which have not deserted my generation.


## 84    Freedom


This mountain standing in the sun.
Out of the light into the heat
out of the heat into the wind
out of the wind into the sun.
Out of the rock onto the snow
out of the shadow of the rock
onto the rock below the peak,
off the rock into shadow.
Freedom cannot be ended.
Out of the snow onto the grass
out of the grass onto the face
out of the grass onto the snow.

93

Freedom cannot be ended.
Out of the cold into the light
out of the heat into the snow
out of the snow onto the grass
and off the grass into the trees
among the trees in the shadow
out of the trees onto the rock.
This mountain standing in the sun.


## 85    The Revolutionary in the Public Park

Three rough-eyed dahlias sting the air like flies.
Thin and wet through and starved of nicotine
the empty hedges wake up shivering.
Melodious birds are in the dripping trees.

And we could outface winter in this mood,
my eyes burn petrol like a steel machine.
I write my name in heaven like one line,
heaven falling apart, snow in the road.

If there are not enough of us this year,
yet I believe that we can never lose
running like time for ever I suppose
breathing as sharp as trees, staining the air.

## 86    History Lesson

Running to fat and rings and yellow silk
a Roman emperor randy with good news
set out his lacquered table under trees
to play with his green ivory chessmen,
while saturnine and tall secretaries
brimstoned papyrus for his metal pen.

One white wood-pigeon with a flashing wing
whirled from the night of the green Roman tree.
The sacred geese left messes on the lawn.
The sentry sun glittered without a blink.
Secretaries hovered. The game was drawn.
A catamite put ice into his drink.

Into the deep, smoke-coloured afternoon
they brought his bed like a loose drift of snow,
he farted, and lay down on it to sleep.
Savages screamed and sweated through his dreams.
Terrified horses galloping breast-deep
kicked at the dead, lashing the icy streams.

## 87    The Master

Schoolmaster, young. He felt his phrases stiff,
plucked from an intellectual wilderness,
wearing his bony peaceful face as if
words were transmuting pain to happiness;
his eyes were gently lighted by success,
one who had drunk his tears and tried his voice
in love of life expressed as moral choice.

Sharp-eyed, ink-grained, a pupil facing him,
grim as a ghost, physical sense and shock,
his jazz was cool and his room-light was dim,
inchoate words, half-truth, a need to mock;
he wore his face as if it were a rock.
The jazz played endlessly without a sound
probing him like a river underground.

This arid thought was worse than anything:
a dry, unreasonable schoolboy mind
distilled through all the levels of meaning,
continuous, insistent, undesigned,
hugging the dark or feeling for it blind;
week after week they worked on one another,
each a *memento mori* to the other.

Week after week dragged into year by year,
each working out his own maturity,
unnatural courage stifling natural fear,
each knowing what he was or he could be
in the degrees of its intensity,
daily rereading one another's eyes
like enemies whom nothing could surprise.

The young schoolmaster rooted into time,
grew rank with blossom, wanted for nothing,
deepened his voice with words caught at their prime,
till working reason and subdued longing
quite ripened and corrupted everything,
watching reflected in the boy's bleakness
the vanity of his own gentleness.

# 88    Landscape with a Wish

When Adam woke without a sound
mountains in his astonished sight
shook off their mist of bluish green,
their ragged sides looked harsh with light,
the air unchipped and purely ground
he feared what naked light might mean.

It means proportion drawn on space
can comprehend water and rock
into intelligence and blood
whose intellectual patterns lock
trees in an economic grace
in human reason like a flood.

Oh autumn heats are finishing—
yellow and red begin to run
among the dark masses of trees,
and the rock withers in the sun;
those cold hilltops are vanishing
to pale colours and fantasies.

And I can only think of this:
I wish this landscape may appear
what blood and mind can make it be,
in the mind's eye its colour clear,
in structure harder than it is,
its lines smoking with industry.

## 89    The Muses

These old women are my muses.
Fruit has fallen behind their eyes.

Look, I can always achieve
the body of an unchristened poem,
I build asleep,
I build it in my sleep.

Is clearer but is bloodier than glass.

But the form of a new poem
is a virgin unearthly diamond
looking up to the sun for the first time.
These worn out women are my true muses.
I believe in the rough skin of their hands,
and the buckets and wash-rags in their hands.

When I have built the form of this poem
may the asthmatic muses christen it.

## 90    Poem in March

At Kew this weather orchids swarm like flies,
stiff wings and silence and a heady smell,
how can such nothings hold themselves so well?
Imitating the artificial skies,
caves of thin-pillared glass surrounding them,
spraying like divers off one turning stem.

*98*

A midland hamlet dribbling down its hill.
Sky scarcely blue. Grass scarcely green.
A touch of river mist scarcely seen.
Houses hardly stone-coloured. Trees still.
Thin sunlight softly brushes in the shape
of pubic woods and feminine landscape.

Builders at work high up printing on air
one economic movement, climbing in
the leafless forest of the scaffolding.
Caging imagined space is their affair,
and gaunt constructed steel is like their own
long legs, rough hands, and cantilevered bone.

Solitude is a casual habit
of yellow grass where the sun comes and goes
loosely among the flapping cloud-shadows,
or mountains drape their tawny flanks in it.
Learn the tougher constructions of the light
building themselves for ever in your sight.

And human life admits this interest,
constructive grace thrusting through everything,
life in the bone and in the eye carving
stem steel and air in movement and at rest.
For things so bare so rhythmic and so tough
I cannot find a word simple enough.

But human life should be what builders are
thrusting their big constructions like a cry
through jointed skeletons of awkward sky
to hang stone-headed in the smoking air:
and the religion of my poetry
is this, what life is or what it could be.

Driving the solid field about sunset,
under a wood half picked out in colour,
I fume coarsely along in the fine air,
thinking how mother earth keeps us at it,
swathed in her withering rose and violet,
her thin liquids, her cold and lasting fire.

Everywhere the same lines show,
tree, cloud, furrow and sky overhead
rounded with seed, leaden as an eyelid,
and everything they promise will come true,
a sky so blue it makes rock look blue,
a wood so green it hides the glittering seed.

The earth knows how to breed and to feed us,
her raw juices are still running at least,
the tractor mumbling at its throatiest
speaks to earth in a kind of lover's voice.
All day like larks we rattle around loose
but twilight finds us fumbling with the breast.

Maker and speaker and machine,
and everything said, everything done
gurgles its gritty pap at this season.
More birds make music than can be seen,
dissolving their sweet names in acid green.
The same heat works on everyone.

I want words whose existence is this,
the rough soil and the root work in them,
praising heaven I ever took for theme
this planet, its unnatural wishes,
common reason and human justice,
and growth of life, the last increase of time.

Words dry, then wither, reason loses hold
in dark intensities of mental cold,
cling to those few whose eye and mind were full
of loud doves in the skull,
tongue-rooted grain and heavily falling fruit:
my words and my wishes
have simplified to this,
to die into a dark more absolute.

I walk by willows knotted up with age,
their crusty trunks and glaucous foliage
painting an image in the still canal:
I wish my eye might fall
deeper by far, the light scum and the brute
and idle swan may ride
my darkness like a tide,
I'd die into a night more absolute.

I lie awake at night in the open,
watch air and dark, hear breaths of wind, rotten
fragments of sky hang down among the trees
blotting their boundaries:
whatever lightest night-time noise the acute
hearing half-wakes to trace
back to its hiding-place,
I'd die into blackness more absolute.

So word by word, and neither fear nor love
can turn aside the darkness I dream of,
the deepest dew, the middle point of night:
go, stumble back to light
that hour when trees stand shivering leaf and root,
and ask them if they might
not shrink from human sight
to die into a dark more absolute.

So word by word poems and conversations
deepen to dark by mutual distillations,
till night itself drowns in a roaring sea,
dissolved into simplicity:
and I must always press into that mute
hive of the dark alone,
where men can be at one
dying in it, with night more absolute.


## 93    Words for a Song

Now all winds and trees engage
like destructive lovers
under the hawk's eye who hovers
in a cold fastidious rage.

On a black untroubled lake
the swan ruffles his wings
creating visible music while he sings
cold songs about shipwreck.


## 94    Fragment

One ageing the other young,
yet it was a single wind
turned their long fingers cold
both the young and the old.

## 95    Poet in Winter

*for Michael Astor*


One candle had a long neck like a swan
straining up from the red tin it stood on,
licking at light with a discoloured head;
it was nothing to look at unlighted:
but light the seven, then look how they shine,
look how they brighten clear or dark green glass,
two on the window-sill will make nine.
Snow deepens outside. Winter will pass.

One meagre constellation edges round
into the mist or drift or underground.
Thick underfoot and final like despair
a whole blizzard of snow peoples the air.
Perseus is huddling stormproof with the goat.
Sixteen candles are burning on my table,
the solemn cries of each extended throat
speak, lament, are starlike, serviceable.

## 96    Poem for Julian

Look out into the snow across the park,
day after day, melancholy beauty,
my poetry will be what it can be,
I take some comfort from the early dark.

As harsh as snow my life is in this room,
and thin and green and tough as a poem,
I write it out often thinking of them,
human poets in whom hope was at home.

Here in the room my speckled orchid heaves
its buds half open, brown-gilt and cream-white,
elaborately floating on the light
out of a thick crop of unbarbered leaves.

Human life could have been as cold as this,
and perfect like heaven, never the same,
flower and leaf by leaf, unwritten name,
some mortal poem as this poem is,

but that humanity is just, discovers
a star dying among the fresh planets,
a darkness in which snow falls and forgets,
covering lovers with the names of lovers.


## 97

The drowsy earth reeking of vegetation
stretches a branch or two, fumbles at spring,
muffles in drifts of cloud, changes position,
sweats, fumes, turns over sleeping:

secure mother, the love of life is this,
and this planet's darling the first one
to break stones in the coarse-grassed wilderness,
to break earth open for grain where there was none.

Wanderers on hilltops religious men
learn this with awkwardness and great affection,
the lie of rocks, cold water's origin,
the slow creeping of moss, the wind's direction.

Pictorial Christ, silent antiquity
has covered them, we must all be silent.
Some birds shouting outside, what intricacy!
the drunken earth stretches, she seems content.


## 98     Landscape with Poet


The level sand the dazzling air
the salt green water the bright sun
had washed him clean of mental fire
he might retire
where rough and dark in line by line
the mountains heaved their craggy spine.
The clouds were trailing blue shadows
as if no noise had ever been,
no one had seen
the opening eye of autumn close.
Bog-myrtle wafted in his nose,
high up he watched a hawk hanging,
two stone-chats hopped from place to place
on the rock-face,
far off he heard a bucket ring;
he held in his reflective eye
the mountains and the mist flying
a hawk striking
the coloured trees the coloured sky.

Around the woods you hear some lost-sounding
cuckoo working on his two rough notes:
so I, whose negative is travelling,
long lost among birds' faces and their throats

can repeat nothing of their argument,
watch and visit as country neighbours do,
comb hedges, spread maps of the continent,
think of music and where it will lead to.

It dries up in the stream at this season,
guttering birds in the coarse foliage
waking from time to time may twitter on,
blank pensioners dreaming a sunshine age.

I am tied down to raft-argosies,
to the owl and badger and rank hedge-parsley,
familiar names of stars and distances,
what the season has been, what it will be.

The celestial globe has dust on it.
No other rose is as simple as this.
Moths in the open might never be hit:
ochre and charcoal as this building is.

And here and there in the bright night unchecked
nightingales will utter their thunderous
first note, growing in air like a perfect
leaf, is as fresh, will be as numerous.

But humanity should have been silent,
is gravel-tongued, its voice is not true,
or else lived in one long drawn out present
talking as friends and as old neighbours do.

## 100    The Poem to its Master

When you were young I flowed upstairs like water
or stood still like an alcoholic drink,
you had never mastered calligraphy
when I ran on your fingers worse than ink.

When you are old you will not be unhappy,
I shall be the element you forget,
time is tolerant of repetitions
the fresh wording and the fresh cigarette.

When you were young I was unmusical,
I drove you in long cars with canvas hoods
or you were rear-gunner, there was no pilot,
and it was me you shot at in the woods.


## 101    Knife-thrower's Girl

Then I was steel,
I was a dark glitter,
my indigo costume the sequin one
was quiet, I was quiet,
felt that I was a long spring uncoiling
high up on one velvet and rhinestone heel.

Then flash, they flashed
left, right, down, left, right,
hard in the wood, up, left, right.
I smiled around, they buried themselves
too fast to be heard, there was I sweating
and breathing only to the front,
felt the mascara running on one eye,
and how I hankered for a wash.

Oh I could eat flowers,
my teeth are natural. Thud, thud.
Round my head. Candied roses.
The eight knives, my eight friends.
The boys are cheering. Walk about a bit.
The worst moment is the moving away.


## 102


In bad weather I imagine a God
like an old man brooding over a kettle
preoccupied with poverty or prison,
careless of families and birds' migrations
and rocks observed by many generations,
but attentive when one line takes its place
on one new prison face.

One can imagine a God like heaven,
disjointed, ominous, particular,
a system maybe, not yet understood,
careless of what ticks in the darkness,
or the wave-motion of human distress,
but waiting for one thing, one magnetic,
hollow, funeral tick.

Thinking about God will not change anything,
and I can no more alter my life now
than change my dreams.
I hope like budding leaves.
I am unable to imagine God.
Hope is a prisoner bruising to death,
green when the life is beaten out of him.

## 103     Science Fiction

(*Contribution to the Shakespeare Festival*)


Dragon-lovers with sweet serious eyes
brood in a desert wood thick with bluebells:
the tough, fire-belching curiosities
mate among ugly smoke and pungent smells.

Seal women linger on the wild foreshore
where in the wrack and footprints of green slime
doe-eyed enormous weed-eaters explore
pebbles and sand, and then begin to climb.

I belong to the Monster Society,
they are my only ramshackle heroes,
I really love them, and whenever I see
monster films I cheer them from the back rows.

I like steam tractors and big, broken machines,
have two old coke bottles on my bookshelf,
I sit through Shakespeare mostly for the scenes
where I am Caliban and love myself.

**Monologue Spoken by the**
**Pet Canary of Pope Pius XII**

Uccello cello cello
I love myself: it seems a dream sometimes
about the water spouting from tree-height,
and voices like a piece of looking-glass.
His shoulder had young pine-needles on it.
At night I used to wake when the big moon
swayed upward like a lighted playing-card,
and someone had uncombed the Great Hallel
with grimy fingers down the window-pane.
I am unable to read their faces
but the inscription like a neon sign
lights understanding in my thoughts and dreams.
The Spirit of God is gigantic:
white wings dripping aether bluer than air.
After I eat I plume myself bright yellow
Uccello cello cello
and hop about on his borrowed finger:
the jewel in the ring without a scratch
and the white silk and the gold thread are mine.
Oh yes, I hop about and love myself.
I do not understand humanity,
their emotions terrify me.
What I like in him is his company
and the long fingers of the Holy Ghost.

## 105    Variations on a
### Theme of Housman

They nod and curtsey and recover when
the wind, when the wind blows:
tall crowds of nettles not unloved by those
who know graveyards, half an eye on heaven

they snuff the air and hope to avoid rain:
behind the vestry some of the dead sleep,
and dried up flowers rot on a rubbish heap.
Whenever rain streamed on the window-pane

he might recall now odorous and dank
the abandoned earth at one with what it covers.
Steaming from rain, nettles brooding on lovers.
Absolute stillness occupies that bank.


## 106    The Upper Lake

Suddenly this morning I saw a pair
of swans snow-coloured above the trees
dropping on loud wings out of blue air
down to the lake between dead rushes;

all morning long they slept and swam,
it seemed a beautiful and moving thing
to one so shadow-minded as I am,
sudden travellers so young-looking.

They circled in the lake current,
ruffled luxuriant wings, and slept again,
then cropped weeds, swept in violent
full flight from end to end of it, and then

*111*

settled back into dark water,
and float there now while owls cry and reply:
around them some reflected stars appear,
pointing the blackness of the bitter sky.

Think of them tonight until late,
white shapes asleep, light-proof, at ease,
or at morning, fresh and delicate,
silent between the cold rushes.


**107**    *for John Holloway*

Two weeks have gone by since I saw the moon:
I have never started a year like this,
it could become annus mirabilis.
Thousands of waves are running onto stone.

The world is visionary and we seem
like flower-eating lover-boys in it,
ice snow mist flame and spirit.
I have lived ten years in a kind of dream.

The woods are stripped and stinging with sea-rain,
a sky like a wounded sea-animal
flies crying by, letting a dribble fall
steady as gunfire on the window-pane.

The Muse is violent with Zeus' light.
On these wild days I think nothing can live
but what is silent and contemplative.
O God, if these days should be budding right.

The world is breaking open in sea-caves,
nothing is there but God and my own bones
and the noise of a thousand, thousand stones
and break-down of a thousand, thousand waves.

These strings of muses weaving among trees
twirling their long scented dresses around
tune their uncomplicated mysteries
into a chorus of enthralling sound

and here am I caught at a loss again
to whom music has never been singing,
understanding a few notes now and then,
hanging about the woods all the morning

straining at their elaborated noise:
I find it too exotic to think of;
we lived wild in the woods when we were boys,
today it tired me out and made me cough.

But thin lamplight will flatter an old muse,
picking about for what was genuine,
shadow-walking, unable to confuse
today's wood with the forest she walks in:

and I can go back to my old obsession,
the thin pages a spirit might write on,
or only he could write whose prepossession
was bare philosophy and religion.

I think of what God loved in Adam,
some plant or some seed of sincere light
live in my eye, which is not what I am,
peasant poet or winter's anchorite:

yet when I lie asleep some time may hear
a few at first then loud and violent
trumpets of silver blasting the sky clear,
treading sleep underfoot, and wake content.

**Thirty Ways of
Drowning in the Sea**

1

The surf breaks. Is never silent.
The wind catches the breathing of the surf,
or catches in the breathing of the surf.
The surf hangs in the hearing of the wind
and is not heard.
The wind is never silent.

2

The sea is deep.
Long columns of a green and salty light
Trail downwards, finger for a floor,
disappear in the sand-coloured water.
I am below them in that deep current
a trailing hand of light will never reach.
Among whose grooves and wards the heavy sea
shifts without turning, like a rusted key.

3

This shadow and this light are in the sea
as massive as the mountains in the air.
What is so black as sea?
What is so black as an underwater mountain
lit only by the stars?
This shadow and this light live in the sea.

4

There is always somewhere the sheer breakdown of a
wave at the foot of a cliff. It takes place somewhere,
the whirls of weed of wood and of wildfire,
the anemone and gravel in the undertow,
somewhere there is the heaving vast and empty
but motionable volume of the sea.


5

Marine glitter,
partly blue, partly green,
and a small, hard smell of marine wrack,
a light taste of pickle.


6

A gull has oiled feathers.
Seeing one, he said
'They are the company a sailor has.'
They are infrequent, I suppose he meant.


7

The sea is a mouthing mythology,
should be held in with mouths of jingling harness,
foams, rolls its eye, flings back its head,
it spreads loose shoulders,
it scatters sand and foam, ungovernable.

8

The sea is breathing. The sea is barren breathing.
The breath of sea is sharper in moonlight.
The breath of sea is not a barren nature.
It is an atmosphere. It is a nature
denser than human life can tolerate.


9

In one season the migratory geese
can paint their breast in pink or in purple,
in vaporous snow-dew, or in sea-spray,
be dusted with the soot of the dead moon,
or crumbs of burning stars or shreds of rain,
repeating in their motion a lost meaning
from the expanses of the moving sea.


10

When I was an adolescent
we walked on every landslide and cliff-top
as if they were an old married woman,
hoarded imagination of gunfire,
stood on breakwaters, had an eye for the sea,
which was extreme and utterly silent,
a mesh of light and mess of foam also,
but magnetic and angry without words.


11

They lie and bake on a rock.
Dusted with metal water round the rock
takes on a deeper colour from the sun.
There should have been a hero:

a girl out of the sea, blowing a shell,
the crab, the oyster and the coelacanth,
*frutti del mare*, dusk underwater.
The empty water ripens in the heat
from bright ink-blue to deeper indigo.
There must have been a hero deeper down.


12

The sea at night in winter.
Colder than black.
Bitterly cold and black.
Water crashes and air roars,
pebbles crumble, the mist reverberates.


13

The young brood of a gull can be skewbald,
the sea also can be light brown and white,
piebald or blue and white or green and white;
when the young gull is tired of the wild air
he drops, settles, rides the seawater;
what choice was brooded in them, if the air
is wilder but the sea more violent?


14

In the end a thing will come to the sea,
granitic refuse, dung of a snow-leopard,
ice, or whatever water can carry,
and tree and house together corroded
by greenery, dying of snow-water,
the dune-grass, the river pebble, the coin
will end in the sea, end in the tide.

15

The intense monotony of the noises,
the ungoverned boom, the loose music,
the toot toot of the isolated bird
cover a nature to be reckoned with,
cold, deaf and barbarous,
in habit rougher than will ever sleep,
calamitous the ultimate applause.


16

Dawn smoking and flaming in the dark.
Disintegrated. But the hussar waves
mimic the angry gunfire of the dawn;
the sea is muffled but is resonant,
I think the whole sea is one thudding thing,
one pure chaos of brinish violence
in whose salt spray the wounded men go down
in ragged water, under firing guns.


17

Over the disused acres of the sea
the wind trolls a bladder of black rain
and my poem is sunk in deep water
under the disused acres of the sea.

18

The diving girl and the diving boy
are deep: blue filters of the sun
fall more coldly than the dark.
These children are utterly naked.
The girl has fish eyes open, his are shut,
she has a flowing tail, his is seaweed,
they turn and turn and turn unquietly,
half shadowlike, half alight in the sea.


19

First morning out
we took on board a shoal of bright herring,
unminted silver wealthy in the net.
That night a gale started,
a living wind, it blew two days,
nothing could have stood up,
till on the fourth morning the sea itself
was wrecked, and we were there in the small boats.


20

And yet the sea is not monotonous.
Hungry-bellied, raucous maturity
will drench heaven, will drown the hemisphere,
and will be tame, but will not be computed.
Monotony, O perfect intervals
of music, but they are not in the sea.
The sea is brutish and has no music.

21

There was a hermit in a wild sea-cliff
whose voice was harsh with holy canticles,
who fed on terns' eggs and on whin-bushes,
his dying spirit fled into the sea . . . .


22

Throw roses in seawater,
crimson freaked with white or green-eyed white,
throw in weighted bushes of ramblers:
they drown dark green or black.
And let them rot where there are no weeds,
brine and the pure air consume them.


23

The ululations of the wind
increasing in the dark moons of midwinter,
the sea roughens, is empty at that time,
disturbed in its whole depth.
All that roaring and not one word spoken.
Waves, insist, insist.
Turmoil voiceless.


24

Flowers are growing under the pine tree,
light or deep they burn darker in the shade:
the wind is sucking at a lemon-skin.
Out at sea many horizons
heave and glitter in their ranks.
Heat. Light. Nature.
Horizon beyond horizon

biting the eyelids like a need to sleep.
We do not understand what we live by;
the sea's cold body is my life I think,
but I have never felt it in a dream.


25

          Now I am caught,
leg, arm, hands and feet,
tugged around in the rough net of the sea,
under cold water like a ton of sand.
The squalling air and the black, wild sea
are eating down the stars of midwinter,
death is caught in the howl of the sea-race.
Dead suns are burning in salt water.
Salt water burns my throat like alcohol.
When shall my body from this death forever
wake with the lash of water in my eyes?


26

The sea stood under a wall of fog,
there was a groundmist in the sea-gardens,
christmas was fumbling with the window-panes.
Sea is stark. The sea was stark.
My cat or hyacinth or cyclamen
stewed to death in the quiet lamplight.
The fog hung in the lines of dripping trees.
Sea rises, lamps drown in their light, and we
must suffer the full fury of the sea.

27

The air is full of mist. The mist is full of sun.
The sea is silent.
Everything has been silent all day.
The old year, the old fire
has been drowned into the fire-eating sea;
nothing but the groundswell can stomach it.
The sea is shameless, it can be silent.
The new year is this small fire in the skies,
gasping down through the mist's infinities.


28

The polished *miserere* dies away.
Here the deep sea is moving between rocks,
fretting itself to marble-paper foam;
deadly as chemistry, and green as tea,
it swirls underfoot at the cliff-base.
But the first sight of the sea
is distant, hanging high up in the air
biting a long horizon from the sky.


29

Capable hands or hard, bare feet.
The Strawberry, the Saint Demetrius,
and the Canary and the Young Lion
put out to sea. The weather is deserted.
I am thinking of the ugliest of stars
half-drowned in night, washed up by bad weather:
they will come back to anchor like that one.
I speak to it. It is not satisfied.
My fatal light is jangling like a chain.
My fatal light is swinging like a chain,
and at the first moments of a morning
the sea catches rough silver from that star.

## 30

The waves rumble clearly,
harsh and deep they swallow their humours.
Gladiators are wading round and round
in blood and sand a muddle in the sky.
The sea is beginning to die.
Sea promontories beat their wings of rock
making the spray fly high from the whipped waves,
the long beaches withdraw in their dark mist,
echo by echo picks out the retreat.
The incessant boom boom gathers volume.
Wherever I move I am in the waves.
The sea is in my ears and in my eyes.

*Ten poems for Nikos Gatsos*


I

Branches of green in trees of darker green

they ran barefoot
they have thrown away their shoes.

Footprint of a star.

I was hungry all night;
I was thirsty all night.
One of them will bring water in her hand,
another will bring berries in his hand

the desert
stirring again
the dust of revolutionary wars.

Sleeping sometimes in the foliage of the vineyard

The darkness hand in hand with the darkness.
I am a secret mountain
tenebrous, flea-bitten by starlight,
my eyes are gone:
then when you cut my throat it bleeds coffee
with a trickle of alcohol.

I am unable to wake
in the vine's thin foliage only fumble
for the dregs of night at the breast of the darkness.

And one hoof of a star printing the dark
is ringing like a nail of a new metal.

## II

Midnight wrings out its withering sunset
I clutch my violet, it smells of garlic
and sleep heavy.
Confusion is bluer than violets.

The law is already an antique:
it is always older than when you woke,
you are unable to say how you know it;
the law is older
             is a given thing
                    and when I wake
waking will be as deep as the dream was

Waking is walking,
is to wake to find
a cold violet coast in a green waste,
where a black horse in bud and a white horse
are chewing down the piebald rose-bushes.

My law is this confusion:
if it were not obscure how could I wake?
The law is an old question
which was over before we were awake.

We woke to find
a white boat rocking on black water
a black wind rocking on white water
a white boat rocking on black water

## III

To speak about the soul.
I wake early. You don't sleep in summer.
In the morning a dead-eyed nightingale is still awake in you.
What has been done and suffered
with whatever is left to be suffered
is in the soul.
Oracles are given elsewhere. Their speech is associated with
  bronze.

In the early morning
you see women walking to the sanctuaries:
a light touch of sun on the whitewash:
a light touch of fire burning the oil.
You tell me nothing.
This is the desert I will write about.
The desert is not an island: the island is not enchanted: and
  the desert is no habitation for men.
The bird with the burnt eyes sang sweetest.
a desert further off
One small simple cloud. Heat at midday. A little constellated
  handwriting. Heat at midnight.

You never say.
To be woken by hearing
the voices of the enchanted birds
and the voices of disenchanted birds.

Say what is like a tree, like a river, like a mountain, a cloud over
  the sun?
My memory has been overshadowed
by that live light and by that dying light.

The soul is no more than human.

The rising sky is as wide as the desert.

# IV

Two hours after waking
and the air already overgrown with coarse grass.
Catch me the little foxes.
Stones and places vary.

These stones and these places
are unattractive to lovers
in the deserts of my imagination poetry is the naked exercise
    of the entire man

its people are not inarticulate
no animal ever leaves a footprint

Light streaming headlong, rivers running sand,
the sweating heads of black and white horses
are beginning to speak.

I was hungry for horse-blood and for horse-sweat.

But listen. They are beginning to speak.
Wild archangels on storming horses trouble
the entire blue canopy of the air.
Music is to be out of tune with them.

The fire and stone-eyed horses shudder their flanks
and speak in gentle, articulate words.

To God, and to the air.

To familiar stones, to familiar places.

## V

Flowers in sand.
There are no footprints in the level sand.
The dune-grass is a rough and hardy green.

Cooling coal smokes on the charred tongue.
The dune-flowers are stiff-looking and white.
Blue coal his dead breath in the freezing mouth.

She is this sand.
One of her hands will hold a reaping-hook.

The sand-flowers are too thin to trample.

Now he is cold;
a stub of candle sticking on one rib.

His mouth is full of burning tobacco.
She heaven-like dissolving into sand,
more stars than sand, more stars than birds,
more birds than rain. It has been raining.

Intermixes with the breath of the sea.

That sand shifting about
will still support a few frail flowers,
bluer than the bluest shadow in her body.

And when I have stood living in this ash
and when I shall stand living


## VI

At night they sleep straight out like the dead.

Their voice is like the black swarming of bees

128

overlooked by hill forts
among the wild, soft barrage of foothills,
discovered early high on the skyline
drowning in the wet, dim purple.

Squeaking birds rouse them in ruined gardens.

and whom the spirit persuades to the wilderness,
or whom the wilderness persuaded to the spirit
persuaded in the wilderness
with others whom the wilderness persuaded

When dusk has scattered its handful of grime
they stream down in the rivers of red flags

Between bones of the sky the sun hangs
and pure and golden
he sharpens up his long blade on the rock.
They glitter in integuments of brass.

They are shadow-scabbed. The brass is curdled.

who have not been confined
into the elements that wasted them,
rust-riveted weapons, discarded whistles,
and bugles in the thick tangle of grass.

You see them always moving. Winter sun
sprinkles the air with solid black and white.

not understanding fortune in the end

fishing for bream contriving their future

and in autumn in the bewildered woods
they lapped the yellow water of the sun
with certain dying stars which ran together
in the dark fields of my nativity.

coarser than a leaf, more lucid than a bird,
not very green

Something is always shifting in the universe.

They are in flight,
dwarfed by the processions of enormous cloud

a lonely motor-cyclist in the sky
look down on cities
stone neck, disproportionate bodies,
unkempt roses, unharvested apples

she offers her big breast without waking

what is the drum-beat of retiring time?
Harshly, loudly, and in the strictest time.

water be clear running over gravel
lead statues absolutely motionless.
He is the only human left alive,
runs with one arm free, swings his lighted
head like a danger-lamp, red in one hand.
This dreadful bird was shrieking in the trees.

Moving about together in the trees.

   In the congregation of young hares at moonrise not a cur
utters and no other creature can keep awake. A night train scat
sparks. Landscape is black and motionable. Dog-bones are mo

their voices carry through the afternoon
they are always learning.
                    they disappear
one by one
            into the circles of the universe,
possessed by forces I have never understood.

They are familiar with cave-journeys and snow-falls.

most dawns are misty

   by evening it has rained, the disillusioned priest and the workmen settle down, black steam obscures the sky

they are moving there

   many ages of faith and some of reason went underfoot to make this breeding-ground.

who came to life under cheerful rose-coloured heavens
and under the rose-coloured and grieving heavens of morning
whose boots were soaked through with field-dew

and the hell of fire will not alter their thoughts

she heaves her green swellings
she trails her brown and yellow kite of vines

in livid metal like a thundercrack
inlaid with yellow and with white metal

and the hell of metal will not alter their thoughts

who alter like the season
whose courage is unnatural
the hell of water is less deep

Look, the liquid movements of a water-rat.

These wood-birds in their winter occupations.

# VII

Under the white stone in the black river
dismembered, waiting for the coming voice

Justice is the beginning of my words.

When the aether was burning in mid-heaven
and every other heaven beyond heaven
had burned itself away,
a drift of cooling soot would cover over
the desert and the burnt-out desert birds

the Law is in flower

small newly given laws are lost already
in a chaos of flowering

And now on the highest, barest hill
the mountain sheep are grazing the sky blue.

No water is fresher or more alive

The Law was never given
but young men
                    and children were found reciting it
their mouths are full of foliage.

Its voice is rocks, wind and the tearing apart of elements.

or you discover
heavy fruit in a multitude of leaf
                    and

the sky is raining soot

Mountainous landscape was not in my words.

God is the Law
and has been newly given
and is in leaf

Powder-crackle
            fire
                    reverberation
are music to my words.
Poetry is burnt out.

It is in the necessity to speak.


VIII

A city built in darkness and cold air

            cold fire

the cold rattle of sparrows and milk-bottles
and early feet already in the street

Towering tomorrows
wade ankle-deep in a groundmist of gardens.

in any man in his life in the meditation of his heart

        your body, my body

There are five pure colours
and one impure religion.

Darkness.
Far away the mountains are snow-speckled.
The shadow edges forward,
it marks the giant doors of the bus station.

    Dressed in blue canvas the nightwind disperses a smell of
rain of diesels and of sleep. This flurry is colder than the last.

wrapped in a heavy coat my younger brother
vanishes quickly in the smoking fog.

This city is a matter of darkness.

uncertain if my brother ever sleeps
what my life is or does what my life is

Fumes of a dying nest of newspapers,
upstairs alone in an abandoned house.

at other times
when the horsechestnuts lighted their candles

clamour of metal in the snow and mist.

their bodies are like water their life summer,
the sunlight will be rumpling everything

We have come back.

Handfuls of leaves are painting a whole street.

                              and in the nettles where
alleys of shadows and humidity
step downward into ranker water-scenes

The stone itself is
the stones are beginning.

The trees have broken into their new youth.
Houses overhanging rivers
                              suddenly
break out into

Ragged red banners are appearing.

   Your body and my body.

   *134*

Last week, at the railway station,
you said. Do you remember.
There was a kind of smoky smell of sun.
For us, to whom nothing has been promised.

I can believe in nothing but in God.

my life is in this belief

my life is in this city


IX

I was asleep in heaven

Now it is evening
and shall we swallow the cup of our life?
I am always thinking about early morning
these woods have been much ruined and confused

The unnatural wilderness of this rock
and loud the echo whistling in the rocks.

Who can consume nature? Who can
consume his nature?
                    That prophet
lies down beside his universe

there are no echoes whistling in the rocks

and light as breath lighter than death it
is magnified by mist and water-spray
sprinkling a green fire and blue scented fire

hardly touches the harsh air into leaf

Emptying out your nature you shall find
a sky that has been hot has been early
is evening how and a certain blackness
is running on the edges of my life

It will be early. I shall wake and hear
the sweet nit-witted chattering of birds

and loud the echoes whistling in the rocks


X

Thousand on thousand spirits in the sun

   I am at the beginning

the blushing birthday roses in my garden

I cannot keep proverbs out of my voice

guttering in the deeper, deeper air

white the sandflowers sprouting among rocks
whose heavy smell is virgin in the rocks

I cannot keep my life out of my voice

one came back from the Asiatic dead
dragging a mass of Asian foliage:
and those with white faces
who rose early, who soberly rehearsed
some few words that had broken greater sleep.

Storm-clouds were cannonading in mid-air.

horses through the mist
                              serpents in the dust

We have drunk dry the voices in the well.

wild fruit
            fresh water
                        those long-legged boys
the nightstick of the sun will batter down
shouting and swearing, stonily

   But underfoot some kind of new grass with a dusky breath.
Moisture, whole threads of aubergines. Yellow and purple, ripe,
ripening.

Or a handful of sparrows at daybreak
coupled again in the rusty scaffolding
break down at night to iron and to stone
the wireless we heard crying in the sun

children's games, lovers' mutterings.

   This spirit was in me.
   I will live in the wind

one who said:
I will eat herbs in the meadows of Glaukos
and live among the dead under the sea,
will feed on honey-cakes and sea-berries,
death and the sea shall herd me with his conch.

Hooters rebounded from Mount Pelion.

Caves will crack and the sea fly apart.

The universe has once been magical

a grain of sugar for the kettle

one who came back
naked under his bronze and linen
his face scarred by planets

this freedom is my theme

green and white comet-tails of fire and ice
trailing into extinction in his eyes

the foxes running on the dead terrace

Daybreak has washed away the dog's print from the dew
these letters from the sand

and shall arise

the second death is deeper than my life

and shall arise
and the moist ringing of a bird-whistle
*alleluiando* in the blackened trees

and shall arise

This freedom is my theme.

**Ruined Abbeys**

*That time of year thou may'st in me behold*
*When yellow leaves, or none, or few do hang*
*Upon those boughs that shake against the cold—*
*Bare ruin'd choirs where late the sweet birds sang.*

Monastic limestone skeleton,
threadbare with simple love of life
speak out your dead language of stone,
the wind's hammer, the sun's knife,
the sweet apple of solitude;
there is a ninth beatitude:
a child in his simplicity
is more than a just man can be.
The idle ruins disregard
a chance human companion,
my words will make little mark on
limestone so jagged and so hard:
places essentially deserted
enchant only the single-hearted.
What are they, sprouting in the trees
dumb and so terrible to see?
What stony intellectual bees
could buzz among such fantasy?
And has my world travelled too far?
Watching all this in an armchair
consider what these ruins are,
desolate spirits in the air
singing in their stone languages
what religion is not and is,
not a museum but a stone
no man can understand alone:
what kind of spirit brought together
all these scattered arches and walls?
and what voice appeals and appalls,
weaving summer and winter weather

into the fabric of a vision,
a silent judge and no decision?

The face of all these stones is dead,
ruins petrify in the trees,
the tower glares like a bald head,
these dead abbeys are fantasies:
like terrible symbolic dreams
nourished on woods and stones and streams,
the dry voice of the river Styx.
Religion wears out its relics.
Their mouths are stone, their eyes are blind,
and who knows what they were saying?
Who can grasp this abandoned thing
pealing like thunder in my mind?
Sometimes I think it is a hymn
shouted by heavy seraphim.

And you might think walking in it
while the pillars move through your eyes
a life, a light seems to visit
a country where it calls and dies,
the truest silence is this noise,
how can that speak which has no voice?
Stone, wind and air without a sound
have risen speaking from the ground.
In the crude dark in the rank air
these clumsy harsh provincial stones
talk loud and clear as megaphones;
it is a virtue to despair
if human language is not this:
what heaven will be and earth is.

What is it in the eye and hand
that makes one thing out of another?
monasteries out of England,
a monk out of a human brother,
bread out of grain in the earth
or a young child out of a birth,

cloisters that could not last for long
from something resistant and strong.
Think what broods out in such a choice,
the ruin human minds intend,
what is this building in the end?
The stone's voice and the water's voice,
ragged walls in the tallest trees
predestined by my first wishes.

My work is like this after all,
to take new life out of a rhyme,
an hour of watch out of nightfall,
to make the day break from dead time,
so the sun's hand in the drowned grass
flashes a hundred panes of glass;
we rebuild night and thoughts of night
into a pyramid of light.
Absolute stillness occupies
the empty vaulted corridors,
the bare feet and the dusty floors
look like a criminal disguise
for secret thoughts and walking late
and that one thing I contemplate.

The pillars are rearing their weight,
the workmen's hands that lifted them
persist as force, to meditate
the discipline of the stone stem:
these stones were in their eyes and face,
their live bodies are this place:
honeycomb of shadows: a city
remote from terror and from pity;
look at the peaceful, soaring motion
like an unmotionable wave,
they never stir in their conclave,
they never speak in their devotion,
but the dead abbey still retains
the dead hand on the limestone reins.

Broken towers push their rough heads
where nothing can climb after them:
sheer arches rest on airy beds
the stone springs upward from the stem:
the eyesight of some holy man
is where this crumpled wall began,
vision and ruin seem the same:
ruin was his nature and name:
pillars like exploding rockets
that draped heaven or stained the moon,
the sting of dark, the swing of noon,
the sun itself and the planets
the empty heavens and the dove—
I understand nothing but love.

But who can understand heaven,
who understands peace of spirit?
What ignorant, what iron men
built this cold place so loving it?
The salmon leaping in his stream
can pull far stronger than a dream,
the black crow against the wind
can climb far higher than the mind.
Who is the man can set his face
to believe heaven will protect
a thing of his own intellect,
a thing of mass, shadow and space?
Confusions in the eye and heart
are where poems, not abbeys start.

The ruins wading through the grass
are like the ghost of Saint Bernard;
as if a thousand years must pass
and the stone face be deeper scarred
before it wakes like a wild creature
into the elements of nature,
might like a swan of heaven sing
its holy note only dying.

Think what brings an abbey to birth
from how deep in prehistory
it took the strong shape you can see,
it seems to have roots in the earth
leaves in the air: but the wind grieves,
it stands empty, there are no leaves.


Ruins are like a strong body
growing its strength in country air
then breeding age until you see
nettles are waving in its hair,
the ruined body keeps its shape
by the mechanics of landscape:
fox in the gorse, wind in the tree,
raincloud, fellside, mystery:
what was born wild is never tame:
ten numbers never written down
can make a spade a wall and a town,
fellsides and abbeys are the same:
until time draws like a deduction
true proportions for their destruction.


Water and stone, bracken and wood,
clouds in the sky, sheep on the fell
have transmuted the true and good:
look close at them and you can tell
the architecture that they like,
think how the sun and wind will strike
at truth and goodness in this shape,
hammering walls too tough to rape.
This world is like a window-pane,
age within age goes its own way:
fields of barley denser than hay
sweep up into long heads of grain
transmuted by his hands who said
the grain will die, my words are bread.

Unquarried rock carries the print
of prehistoric origins,
the burnt forest sleeps in the flint
and the worked stone builds the ruins;
what ice, what mountain weight of ice
compounded rock in this crevice?
What glacier groaned in the lock
to lock this strength into this rock?
Streaming with water, secretly
breathing the cold eating the sun
until its prison was undone
by Christ in the twelfth century,
this rock endured, and you can trace
the hurt hands in the quarried face.

Bones are a limestone but it bleeds,
a man is an imperfect stone,
what the unquarried limestone needs
is intellectual alone,
it can sing louder than a thrush
on the fellside in the rose-bush,
without a clapper like a bell,
as clear as Christ in the gospel:
all creatures breed with their own kinds,
and when this rock was remarried
Christ and the gospel blessed its seed
with *amor vincit*, love binds.
What is it in the marks you see
so moves you to morality?

Think how high a pillar can stand,
primitive art, a kind of zero,
still the work of somebody's hand:
a self-portrait, a limestone hero,
a fantasy drawn in the light,
expressing self-knowledge as height:
and stone on stone:—this discipline
has a deep limestone origin.

Only the virgin stone knows why
the arches swing against the sky.
We use ruins for idle time
to take a bath in the sublime.

This abbey was what the tree is
and the column is natural,
now its branches are silences:
*e'en let it stand till it down fall.*
Angels like birds caught in mid-flight
were incoherent at twilight;
birds are dead meteors, this age
puts out no stony foliage,
but my face is a figurehead
split by the weather in the south,
the stone ivy twines in my mouth,
angels are finished, birds are dead:
and yet the ivy on the tree
is my life, is what I shall be.

Deep in the woods masses of leaves
live as no abbey is alive,
the unprinted sunrise receives
its praise only from crops that thrive.
Monasteries in their November
can only mumble and remember
this sharpness in the life and sense:
life is some kind of innocence.
Natural uses and abuses
eat down the forest in the end,
and only stone is the stone's friend,
distilling solitary juices:
heaven revives and lives forever,
the end of religion is never.

Night stalks through the ruins.
Moonlight and dusk handle relics.
The river remembers its sins.
Things interpenetrate and mix.

The old sunk ship rises up high
disturbing birds in the black sky.
You are yourself at night, prophetic
in your nature, and sympathetic
to forgotten laws of childhood,
night is your natural limit,
this body of darkness in it
is your extreme of solitude.
The abbey at night is a king,
an unexampled, solemn thing.


And this darkness never deludes.
It is original justice,
the Buddha of these solitudes;
riches too cold for avarice.
This is the original mark.
Monks like bees buzzed in the dark,
they were moths in a black forest
where the tree-sugar ran truest.
This is intellectual light:
day-working and night-waking,
the psalms sung with their eyes aching
the human darkness and midnight:
the bees of darkness in the hive
of light when the light was alive.


An absence and a poverty:
a certain simple understanding
of what a man is or will be,
ears and eyes for the one commanding
face with the gaze of fire that looks
out from the first Christian books.
Something human opens at night
and grows slowly towards the light.
It dawns. Birds call for daybreak,
stop singing, and the world's awake.

146

Bread of heaven, heavenly light
shake away sleep from my eyes,
make the sun flame, the day be bright,
O light, O darkness of the wise.
This abbey is stones and ashes;
I no longer know what it is.
Dead monuments. An extinct fire.
It has neither voice nor desire.
Say at one particular moment
which old history had prepared
and many generations shared
this abbey element by element
was desecrated beyond all mention
and the fire smothered and the hearth pissed on.

Try; break the walls up in your head,
let cattle-urine splash the chrism,
see the place well desecrated,
safe for art history and capitalism;
and then remember in the end
that all of this really happened.
But that the intonation of the wind
is savage, and it is not in the mind.
We live at the whole world's expense,
we live in debt, what was rejected
can not ever be resurrected.
Never. There is no innocence.
In this generations will share:
a dead abbey is a nightmare.

Look at this and be terrified,
it was not the judgement of God,
it was not sloth, or wealth, or pride,
but a choice taken and followed.

Peace is a bird in mid-heaven
that can be known by lonely men.

This lonely and abandoned house
whose voices no voice can arouse
visited for an hour or two
will say in Latin *meditate*,
and recites phrases like *too late*
to those who know what they should do.
Well, forget the abandoned crime:
live better in the present time

What is it then, a human
life, human society?
The Bible says four streams ran
from paradise; where are we?
Body, spirit, Holy Ghost,
the language is dumb almost.
Who really knows his origin
or whose image we are made in?
Adam was sweating and digging
three centuries in paradise;
I sweat and dig for the same price,
and sing as loud as the birds sing;
but this is not the first garden;
monastic heaven is broken.

When Adam worked in the sun
his tree was lost, he hated light,
he loved shade, so he grew one
like a fresh garden of delight:
Adam was nine hundred and blind
when this great tree grew in his mind.
All those paradises are over.
Work goes on. There is no cover.
I have this simple attitude:
God gives the tree, waters the root,
God gives the tree and the fruit,
the fresh apple of solitude.
Say what is a human spirit?
God gives the bread that feeds it.

Spirit in heaven, white dove
inspire what God has created,
with water-springs of heaven's love
till soberly intoxicated
I can see my own origin,
the unknown image I am in.
The dove of heaven is alone,
his breasts are water his voice stone,
once in history he defied
nature and man for a virgin
building his streams for ever in
the snowy heaven of her side;
every monk and abbey is
a kind of monument of this.

It ends in death, the old land.
Darkness climbs into the sky.
There is nothing left in your hand.
It gives you no guide to go by.
Or nothing that a stinging-nettle
on a bleak stone will not unsettle.
You who believe my true story
are not protected from history.
What can I say about death;
their death is hidden from my eyes:
but I believe that the dead rise,
having been roused by the strong breath
of my God who is in heaven,
when the trumpet tears earth open.

Before they died death was present,
in such a death all life survives,
this is to die human and content,
at peace and delightful in their lives:
and there was nothing lamentable,
even death can be serviceable.
Under the earthly limestone crown
in grave after grave they lay down.

Here death was never quite at home,
in fields not chosen for dying
they simply slept and lie sleeping
and shall lie till the crack of doom.
And I hope to be one who dies
with simple ruins in his eyes.

Water is running in my head
cold as the water from Christ's side,
cold as the voices of the dead
and of those who have never died,
they live in words, they are still speaking,
they have found what I have been seeking.
Ailred of Rievaulx and Bernard,
was it only on wood so hard
your ripe, sound apples could grow?
Under the coarseness of time
under lichen, rain, grime,
ruins are all that I know:
and your words speaking from the page;
the Word is in words, age after age.

The rain has blotted out the stone.
Try to understand its message.
I take the stone's life for my own
these ruins for a hermitage:
here I shall contemplate that truth
which must consume my age and youth,
and put words to that only good
that chimes so well with solitude.
The foolish letters of poor names
are written on this holy stone,
but reading them I am at one
with the Arabian bird in flames:
death in the amber-weeping tree
whose life is what my life shall be.

(*for a B.B.C. film of Cistercian ruins in Yorkshire*)

**112**

Red goes grey, hangs dripping in the trees:
lucidity, the autumnal bird-whistle.
A supreme fiction is to create light,
fiction is to create and love someone.
Unspoken poem, mother of my muse.
The white flower is softer than the light.
I sit here eating poetry and grass.
So many unripe pears, so many sharp leaves.
In many languages of foliage,
in dream after dream, in beginnings:
am lucid only when I am asleep.
The true and good in written poetry.

**113**

It was the chestnut tree by the fire station
that used to colour; nutting in August,
shooting at birds in intricate bushes
while the fruit fell and the rough leaves hung on:

we used to move by instinct and a smell:
stubble was time, afternoon was airguns
and earth, hedges, it can't have been clouds
were the only thing in that life that ran well.

Friend of suburban children, communism,
for whom life seemed to run clear in the end,
the wireless music and the cracked veneer
were muddy dregs inside the microcosm.

Who can break loose without a sense of sin?
There was no discipline except living
reason confused, what was obscure was free,
drumbeat of words was the one discipline.

Suburban streets are a kind of forest,
in which religion is the darkest place,
and early morning the one naked thing;
you lived by bird-whistles and built your nest.

Most of the fruit was coffined, asleep, dead,
there was a lack of clanging in mid-air,
the beach pebbles were tan and flint and white,
we disappeared but nothing had been said.


## 114


Sleeping unquietly I dreamed of sleeping.
The man who has not invented his life
knows better what it was he had to say.

All night he was a swan of peace and murk,
night, month and year the river extended,
swans in the woods the river in winter.

Then all morning he lay in bed afraid
because bare sky is the most living thing,
windows of light paced around his room.

The cherry and pear tree in blossom mean
cold fingers and fine grass and fine rain.
The garden is thorn trees, violet webs.
But when the light climbs it is mere blue.
Without dregs it is standing in his eyes.

**115**

Omens in the pear trees and in the mist.
Continual winters sicken the mind
with voice after voice of wind after wind,
hammers as cold and black as they can be.
Blue and gold the cold air of tomorrow
waits for the mason's gang and line of sky
that will dangle rough fruit in the green tree.


**116    When the Rope Broke**

There was this rope-end trailing over him.
It whipped and snapped. The light scalded his eyes.
The mountain swung around him in the air
and rock by rock broke outwards from his hand.
At dusk they found him pale and loosely lying
grasping and grasping in his silent mind
at five enormous thistles, two stonechats
and between eddies of the mountain mist
deep-feathered hawks on burning bracken wing,
slate-coloured water mountain darkening.

*for Iain Watson*

Lingering time itself records itself,—
think time is over, say goodbye to it;
bird after bird expires into belief,
the sun among the stationary trees
touches the blue to level green and white:
there are no riddles in remarks like these.

Some of the young are poets I suppose
picking about in one another's lines
cobwebbing their own eyesight in shadows:
austere nature has ways to execute
the lively figures of her rough designs,
time is their voice and nature strikes them mute.

Time moves among the frosty rushes where
the daylight dies out with a rasping sound,—
these are the shortest days of the whole year,
trailing from fog to fog through seas of dew;
the ruffled birds desert the startled ground,
streams run in chains of ice, and weeds grow few.

Think time is over, say goodbye to it,
taking new words to make a new season;
draw bleak horizons working by lamplight,
and let your eyes rest with a new surprise
on men and steel and jobs they use it on
and on the wild birds settling in their eyes.

**118**

Machiavelli's evil role
was loving the state more than his soul;
having no soul to give away
would be the best role in the play.

**119**

A dog barked in the night. Somewhere a lamp
shone through mist or a train was passing.
All that air, all that darkness
fuming with weeds and the quiet canals.
And what is it that aches and endures?
A train breaks open the black distances,
cold air, the taint of cinders and of leaves
infects my tongue. Awake before morning.
Not a mouse. Not a bird.
Last night two violins on the wireless
like rivers too cold for the swan to breed.
Rivers in Poland and in Germany
have left smells on my body and my hair.
You ask, Will there be peace before Christmas?
We travel on. The garden
is unable to speak, able to speak.

The long train swings. In carriages alone
we dip cold faces in sweet-smelling prose
are ignorant of the world I suppose,
the journey wears us inward to the bone.

Honey and darkness and a private thought.
Saffron to blue. The New Year come and gone.
Each morning sky shipwrecks the Parthenon.
Girls in the trees Apollo never caught.

Feed on some molten drippings of the sun,
wheel in the wind, the glittering dark blue
of the wild sea, canaries singing true
all day in prison in deserts of stone.

The sea marries its island in the end:
the waterfront shakes out in a long line
saying one name, there are glasses of fine
basil and a few roses have ripened.

Paint up your crumbling house, live there alone,
cape and rock magnify in the dry light,
the ragged sea breaks to a dazzling white;
thrushes twitter in the whale's skeleton.

If you or I could see
the south of Italy
when it was pure forest
and uneroded rocks
were green and silver clocks,
a shallow grassy breast,

when there was no rock chapel,
when the delicious apple
of technics was unbitten,
suppose there was no doubt,
nothing to write about,
and nothing had been written:

should we have crossed the stream
from the nightmare or dream,
kicking up spray around us?
Sleep-people who are all
human, all animal,
would I suppose have found us.

Should we have built tree-huts
among the sweet chestnuts
or dug deep hiding-places?
Need it have ever ceased,
the beast-god and god-beast,
stub horns, enquiring faces?

Urbanity the note,
the sea-foam-purple throat
pulling the heroes in?
Could I have done much better
than this poem and letter
and map to travel in?

The dead world in the trees
has drier mysteries
than the dry year's death-rattle;
trees among trees in leaf
look like a dead belief
after an autumn battle.

Do you and I suppose
white rock with blue shadows,
the cold ash of the ages,
and stunted second growth,
broken up land, uncouth
caverns and hermitages

are really what arouses
mosquitoes and mean houses,
mad dogs, abandoned metal?
The truth is what we see;
what grows is Italy:
the dust will never settle.

Further away the Greek
mountains from peak to peak
climb their amazing lines,
and if they wreck the sun
the blood of air will run
bluer than when it shines.

Only we get the grace
to write in such a place
who can never forgive:
and learning how to hate
write chiefly for a time
when the sweet wish to live
will have died out in it.

## 122

All that weight of stone and of brick
rearing and toppling in my father's dreams
and the black-shadowed ruins in his times
have buried my life though I am awake,

now after years the landslide is moving
I have learned how to hope delicately
for some light fur of grass and a fruit tree
to fear no one to be sure of nothing.

I say the sea is in: the new spirit
is bluer than knowledge or industry,
weed-green for life, art will be swept away,
in our lives Europe is saying goodnight.

Despair is not in the intellect,
it is experience not a belief,
bitterness is a kind of forgiving,
and I am freedom's lover and addict.

## 123

The break of day and the falling of night
birds fish moths in their generations
come without date: there is no infinite:
sea, rock and fossil are my creations.

Poetry without time is a sun-flame
flickering on the misty sea-surface
conversation has always been the same,
seen naked its body has strength and grace:

and I consider I have no future
but sea-blasted roses and foreshore grass,
the strongest languages are most impure,
I wear love on my chest like a horse-brass.

O unwritten poem, secret mountain
peaks, bogmyrtle, bracken and idle men,
handfuls of birds in handfuls of rain,
repeat these words once and forget them then.


## 124


Smoke when the sun fell and when it rose,
girls in their fresh white stinking of jasmine
women on mules their mouths smelling of wine;
the children played on dusty pianos.

Winter, you can remember backwards to
cigars and dying apples in the mist;
tunes and bad weather like a hand at whist,
I shift barley too dusty to see through.

Dreaming you can no longer understand
these times although they fall like a footfall,
now to wake is a kind of refusal,
anemones wake stone-cold in your hand.

The confused breasts of so many mountains,
too much rock, who can understand it?
One gulf is silver the sun fingers it
like a boy with a whistle while it rains.

No clock strikes with a perfectly clear chime,
dogs and lorry engines wake up together.
Dying women can prophesy the weather.
But I shall not be awake at that time.

## 125 St Valentine's Day

Hungry doves in a parliament of birds
shiver with love: their white communities
express a kind of gurgled discontent
through pouted breast, wild eyes and wheezy song:
and all thrushes call imprudently loud
breaking a hush from hillside to hillside,
that kind of music is no argument.
But the blinded, imprisoned nightingale,
the small canary and the quayside greenfinch
will infinitely vary one complaint
until dead shadows hang like draperies
over the heads of the birds' parliament.
Yet I know that the strongest and angriest
bird is the lover swan in his movement.

**126**

Snowy wars, snow-muffled fruit trees,
a clear moment, a long, bellowing train:
this coughing on the platform, this cognac,
the reeds and floods, the city in the rain,
the prison wall, you can never go back.

Say what it was, what were you looking for
in the darkness, in the trees, in the cold?
My brother who has for so long understood
the fruit on the fruit trees and is lost now.
Reading all night you get cold, you get cold.
The Rome express goes screaming through the wood.

They burnt it down in nineteen forty one.
Why is the wind dry and the dawn dry?
Darkness is in my mind; it is his time;
a musty smell where the birds have nested,
green bushes where the birds will not reply.
The station lamps light you enough really.
Roses have eaten them. This was my crime.

**127**   *for Joan and Paddy*

Fifty years ago I might have died.
Nothing is growing in the villages
but scraggy wheat: *ploutos* repurified.
The children are in leaf darker than trees.
I think there are bare voices in the stars.
The mutterings of those cold fires are wars.

Something died and has come alive in us,
it withers cobble stones and old railings;
beautiful poverty was victorious,
I am fighting the coherence of things.
All my true-seeming words will shake to pieces
when my lamp dies and the dawn cold increases.

Labouring all night on the moon's dark side
I built an iron train: that train is full;
but might have died where Agamemnon died
slowly threshing the water like a gull,
and am in love with cuttings in the rock
where the muse cuckoos like a cuckoo clock.

I have built nothing in thirty-five years
except five wooden gates into a wood.
I sweated mist, beach pebbles were my tears,
red and white dawns which I have understood
broke into cold, and dried up in the end.
The people have no flag left to defend.

There is nothing in providence but leaves,
there is nothing in my heaven but stone;
no one in mountain villages believes
what I believe when I am alone;
the hammer strikes again and again,
it is the gold and silver age again.

Men are like birds and have their building times,
a man's wing will be free and his cheek red,
birds in his hand, not anything that rhymes,
sparkshowers shadows metal compacted,
a note so true that not one bird can sound it,
but whole ages of years stand still around it.

Pebbles, ashes, swill of the black water,
the rain flashed lightning, smelt of kitchen herbs,
it thundered on that night, you were awake
banging the iron blanket, one free hand
like fire burning without wires in the air,
the sea, the wind, the whistle and the roar.

Washed up. The waves are slamming their green door
And the wrecked sea still riding in the sky
crowded with lilac till late afternoon,
we were tied to the yellow riding light:
foundered: your eye the darkest it has been
and your breath rougher than the surf's cold breath.

Stepping out say like trees through blue daylight
my groin tangled in leaves I am freedom;
generations of red and white water birds,
that strong dark green, how quickly a fish dies,
pitching across the jetty like a deck,
the whitest lightning I have ever seen.

Season there can be no resurrection.
Do not die, do not believe in death,
good God, you are as pure as a sea-pebble
sinking into sea-ashes in the sea.
I tell you in that storm nothing can live
but what is without life, and true, and free.

Drowsy tree. In the end it revives
and the sky suddenly begins to flash
scattering masses of the mist and leaves;
abundant pure smells, then the thundercrash:
Apollo barks, the god's in his machine,
the light is mine and the darkness is mine.

The last calamity is love of life,
it is my only tears, the ghost of God
wears away nature, live by this belief,
it wears us down, the darkness is wasted,
night birds like shreds of dawn are repeating
nothing, the cold the light sweats is nothing.

Look now. The buckling wheels of the sun's car
drop shadows of metal on the dead men:
there are wild birds whose voices express fear
who will not abandon my body then;
it is the kindly work of the rock-dove
to drop pure water in the mouth of love.

The moral dark of poems is over,
they set to impenetrable crystal:
batlight, the moon's detritus running clear,
the stars' burnt feathers hissing as they fall;
listen: it is the Word with scything wings
purging the sky of his imaginings.

God is soughing in the country silence.
It is common to love one another.
When the sun rises it troubles my sense.
That smoky redness is God in his fire.
There was no one else: therefore the prophet.
Speaking in words the rock-face will forget.

## 130

And a lost summer at a dying point
woods enough hills enough and words enough:
weeds, the dank humus and one eye of light.
Trees and words look loosely. They were not meant.
What is not loose and cannot speak is love.

Out in the miles-long looking fields of grain
one tanned roebuck as dark as a raincloud
running like death, freedom is untrodden,
the ragged trees are a dark battle-line
gunning the tattered air over the road.

There is still something in the exhausted soil
clean of association, will break clear,
like a late river cloudier than steel
where avenues of leaves coil and uncoil,
like night grass, and fireworms as cold as fear.

What is not loose and cannot speak is love.
Not what she is but she is what they are.
I will be the mad hermit of these woods,
life is a coarse language, it shall be love,
I say nothing shall speak but what they are.

## 131

This fire that walked ankle-deep in the sea
confusing stones and fringes of the sea
was God's fire. There are seasons in your mind.
So few stones. Nothing I understand.
Always like this, dumbfounded by the sea.

You drop shadows on my page of long lines.
There is no rest in God and his designs.
My poetry is the dumbness of life:
buds of darkness, tree-blossoms of belief,
and the cloud-bird, his long and longer lines,

crying inward through rainy atmospheres:
there is not so strange music in the spheres.
I am silence, and these voices will die.
There is pure fire in God and in his eye;
the sea revives through fiery atmospheres.

Your mind is words ripped off from air and light,
night smells of branches in the sea and light:
there is no fire in my understanding:
dark leaf of life: there is no forgiving
the coldness of breath when it becomes light.

## 132

Then one day by the window in the new place,
to sniff the tree-line, hear an obscure thrush,
lifts open something inside the whole sky,
this ruffle-feathered bird in a rank bush
proclaims I love, I do not love, and why.

No one understands these beginnings,
the beginning of daylight, the apple-blush
declines yellow, the rough and heavy sea
dies and is revelation and the thrush
will say I cannot love, love is in me.

White drops of fire hang crazy overhead:
what time has begun, what life will finish.
The raving of the bird in the dawn-flush
was language and it is a dying wish:
it is the new ruins, the desert grass.

## 133

It happened. A head bleeding on a high pole.
The sea quietly makes in, appears to lap
sweet liquors, green spheres on the table-cloth,
like the low hum of an important conversation.
Little swell, a provincial reputation.
The waves slam like trump after trump.
The patent shoe, the plastic cuff, the army
in leather and in linen. Heavy steel.
Waves pouring over that machinery.
There will be salt in the sky on that morning.

## 134    Song

O simple love
this happy man
will not lie down
and be alone
until in death
he must lie down
O simple life

## 135

Nothing has been written about this life.
I am a glacier, I am a rose
as blonde as honey smells of narcissus,
cattle-eyed, the skin dusty but not rough;
white trees are mysteries, the wood is life.

I can tell you this whole wood is bare trees:
what you can smell is the greenness of must
and a white solid blanket of groundmist,
heavy sleep is the best I can advise
then become wooden-breasted like the trees.

This bible hermit has his kind of life:
his reward is to live thirty years wild
crouching in grass like a hare in a field;
trickles of rain give him water enough,
the truth of his bible is in his life.

## 136

The sky cleared and we came to an island
fresher than daisies greener than sunshine
the mountain spouted fire, it was God's land.

We saw a virgin standing in the cave
greener than daisies fresher than sunshine
her shadows and that fruit are all we have.
The storm has not cleared. We are in the storm.

One day was clear, the evening gilt and green,
shooting long shadows, it could mean no harm,
the sea will be where the island has been.
It is dark now. We use life in the storm.

**137**

When does it end? When does a new poem
ever end? It ends with the island.

Boats, where green watered Puritanic sand
carries offshore beyond the twelve mile limit
yelp and squall of the wind, musk of the girls,
the sailor knew his sweetheart in that wind.

We move through sleep, silently and alone.
Then rises to the surface glowering
it is a tree growing
a lyric poem will have no deadline.

The wrapped roses smelling of paper
are pure explosions of reason
and have no end to them. Modern times;
we are some kind of lover in the end.

I love those most who have no role in life.
        Nothing awake.

Poetry is reason, a slow coming awake.
The world was waiting for lyric poems.
Reasons conjoined, work of the body,
and language cannot be sweetened
but freedom is the burning cigarette
on everyone's lips.
The word of reason when it is awake.

Time's harvest is not in the loose life of my dreams
island beyond island beyond island

when I am awake.

The bombs are finished.
It is silent.
We live hanging two or three hours in mid-air
in seats of steel like birdmen in childhood.
They disappeared into the cold.
Flamed in the misty nostrils of the sun.
How many villages?
I am holding on to my hat.
Can you say what these people will do now?

The Captain scribbled, covering his hand,
Maybe I am the silence.

This paper is thirty prison islands.

Freedom torn into pieces in my hat.
Look. I shall empty this hat in the hedge.
Purer than water and stronger than grass.

Tree of roses. The water crashed headlong
tearing the darkness out of the stone face.
A god of war might be a god of song.
The sign of faith is a physical grace:
thinness colour and smell like Asian clover,
the informal appearance of a lover.
Water is religion, it has no voice,
but drowns the silence of God in its noise.
There is no life to be had in the pure air,
and passion for goodness not having it
is rank swan-music and water-spirit.
Ice and a hundred moving points of fire:
the monks in the illuminated cave
only love what cannot love and will save.

In England morning colours like fruit-skin,
it darkens again with a whisp of light:
apple-trees to work at, grass to play in,
the blossom in the deepest woods is white.
That sun is cultivated, the sky even:
the god of song can love nothing but heaven.
He is exploding stars, the piston-rod
in the sky's dying engine, true and good.
His sudden, light drumming in a back street:
what passes is love, it is not belief,
love's religion is destructive of life
it is the heavy seed in the pale wheat.
Death shakes out the last words, what they release
is the old god of nature and of peace.

Living in the religion of peace
where God is outward, the world ingrowing,
I break my life to pieces in my voice,
to be like God in his imagining:

the origin of goodness was a fable
piety cast off made it available:
passion for goodness is love in the end,
it is broken language nothing can mend.
The throaty agitation of the trees,
snowinfected, colourstained by the air,
expresses green nature like a despair:
whatever lives has inward boundaries.
God has none, he is natured like a stone
frosteaten and sunbitten and alone.

## 140     Riddle

Without me there is no person.
You would die by what I live on.
Thistles can be a skeleton.
The element of rock is height,
the broken rocks I cannot eat are my delight.

My limbs are chaos in motion,
the dusty coat, the dead lion,
my breath was sugar, it is gone.
The element is dry and bright,
the broken rocks I cannot eat are my delight.

The blue immense murdered my swan
my yellow and my green and brown.
Blind I am cold, my eye is sun,
I have voices that live on light,
the broken rocks I cannot eat are my delight.

**141**

Wooroo of wild birds in a ragged garden.
A gunshot hardly motions them at all
banging away at sixpence in the wall.
I choose peace, and the dumbness of this season.

The pink weeds in midriver on the island
and the thin poplar woods are without weight,
air scored with branches, branches scored with light,
walnut and willow give the sun day-shadow.

It has a house maybe of a rough texture,
hollyhocks and great sarsens of granite
(splashed ochre and a kind of silver-white)
decorate the rough hills time hardly grazes.

Things pile up an analogous confusion;
these old sunflowers hallooing the sun
extend themselves as if death were someone,
or snowy quiet not the one dimension.

**142**

Bushroses hanging crumpled a leaf drops,
time is new extent minute by minute,
lives easily in wet, dark middle air,
green fruit will hang stains of colour on it.

Age-ease is no profound intuition,
it is dark extent, future memory,
can move freely in the horizon of one hour:
spirit is breath, lighter than time can be.

Buddha is in nature, in my nature,
and silver and solid as a time-piece:
the richness in the Victorian dark;
the sun's whisper troubles Buddha's increase.

Full snow-rivers tear away the whole track,
rock-dust withers and it is sediment.
Poplar and willow make light architecture,
and green embroidery on the blue tent.


## 143


The stain is in my liver and my brains
and my strength is a carcase of soupbones.
Heaven is swirling like a summer cloud,
there is no salt in the weak taste of blood,
the spirit blows to tatters in thin trees
and whines and cannot reach the provinces.
The angry mewing of the party chief
sours the bloodbath by indicating if.
He will become paper, become God,
a paper taste alternative to blood.

## 144

Against this there is no poem then.
Big mountainsides where the small sheep are creeping,
mosswater weeping,
will see the end of Christ and his brethren.

The last trumpet: it is guerrilla war,
the one-eyed helicopters have gone hunting,
the deer are drunken
and I am drunk on the light breath of this star.

God changes what humans are conscious of,
we are old children, glass is our essence,
we give acceptance,
we know prisons, we are conscious of love.

## 145

Growing mint is a pleasure of penance.
When I was twenty-five I was in France,
I saw nothing naked and virginal,
nor did I play tennis, nor ever shall.

Flowerpots of red and white double stock
are political issues, I am still on the hook.
Watering cans and string are a mystery
to me, but this is the honey in history.

I am wagging my tongue like an animal,
in theatres there is no music at all,
in the past world lilac was ordinary,
may mornings, what you could smell, what you could see.

Sigh and roar! Night is your continent,
grass under moon, the simple and decent,
where what is virginal in the coming world
feeds in the dark; it is still crisp and cold.

## 146

Summer is winter, spring will be autumn.
The fruit of the pear tree and apple tree
make the brown hooknosed eagle roll his eyes
to meet the mild eyes of the English dove.

## 147    Ballad

Under the hollow hooves of the rough-coated ponies
a lost valley muttering to an audience of mountains,
stranded in a wild country in the month of midnight
Phyllis was running, running after Corydon.

Loosely behind the light hooves of the night-coated horses
thunder sighed in the heather to an audience of mountains,
through a perpetual autumn of rocks rivers were raving,
Phyllis went crying, calling after Corydon.

Under the liquid hooves of the advancing, circling riders
one bird screamed in the grass to an audience of mountains,
lost in the shivering daylight, tired of the barren starlight
Phyllis ran screaming, screaming after Corydon.

Louder than the crashing hooves of the enormous riders
the sky cracked, birds were silent, rain tumbled in torrents,
in the vast grottoes of loneliness and the green caves of sorrow
Phyllis went weeping, weeping to an audience of mountains.

Quiet. The light, beautiful thunder of the receding horses;
Corydon stirred in his death like the flowering plants in the ocean.
In a never-ending country where all the trees are uneasy,
white and cold and dead under an audience of mountains.

## 148

This spasm when I write and the disorder of my dreams,
this *tremor cordis* in the newspapers, wordy extremes,
all these bell-tones and noises chime the age away,
and God will make them come true in the street one day.
There is heaven in the destruction of this star,
and some philosophy where peace and pleasure are.
I say in the kingdom of the blind music is king
but liberty, reason and life have the most meaning.
Eighteen forty eight and nineteen fourteen
have blotted out democracy as if it had never been.
I say we shall see that generation again.
And God shall fulfil this with his amen.

## 149　Greek Folksong

On an apple, sweet apple, heavy apple tree
a hawk was searching in the branches of an apple tree.

'I want to build a nest in your branches, apple tree.'
'Fine feathered hawk, such a thing cannot be,
you are scattering my blossom and the fruit drops out of me.'

New groves of rough blue heads. Thin. Wild. The sun
    has not been absent.
Nor the rain in ruffled feathers.

In clouded farms, on cobbled yards, among the loose dung
    and the warm straw smelling of horse-piss, walks
    one white pigeon.
for poetry to be quiet
your hair is rougher than wool

O my unwritten poem, old and white biplane
nature was self-consumed and unforeseen: I beach
    my boat and paint it up in winter,
so savage as a moth
outlive the gudgeon in his humid palaces
the willow is the English olive-tree

                there will be fog in march
in wild grass where it takes an acre to keep a peewit and
    the water soaks your boots and larks rose shivering

                God in the stonès
and religion was not a matter of nakedness.

He has gone, leaving written papers.
To many houses, all stone and sky,
some green growth in summer, some deep snow in spring.
Thousands of words of dream scribbled on a bedsheet.
This man tore down the fruit from solitude unripe.

In these woods, in the first leaf of the elm
when stone becomes shadow
the most tormented mind is motionable
it will be stony,
can settle among trees like an enormous butterfly
and shadow becomes stone.

Has gone away through the woods.
Where you hear birds now and then.
Small bodies, shrill voices,
a hundred juliets in balconies of branches.
Indoors at night the yellow globe
illuminating nothing.
Words written in the light of death.
It measures time, ripens without falling.
By now has gone a long way through the woods.

He is above the snowline,
in yellow and white clouds swirling marble
coughed out a star a tiny speck of blood.
You cannot know. You only know that he went on.
Am in this poem like a monastery
inscribing words on air and on darkness,
with the texture of rocks and villages
and the sea's unripeness.

Which is neither mine nor his, but in common.

I imagine where God has never been
and a landscape Adam has never seen,
say a broad estuary
crab-apple salty on the crooked bough
different from the places we live now;

and I imagine by that estuary
and grape colours and long tones of the sea
quite a new kind of poem
without excuses: thistle, sand and reed
are their own explanation like the creed.

Inland birds cannot enter the poem,
because they carry an intense light with them,
streams of old-fashioned skies;
and half human bird-noises will not fit:
night falls heavy, seabirds understand it.

When traffic died I dreamed the other night
about a god with sheepskin wig and tight
violet breeches writing * * * *, and then
satiric verses with a golden pen.
And God knows what the art of satire is,
I wish I had metallic breath like his,
the only metal in my constitution
is if you talk about a revolution
a knife gets whetted on a stone somewhere
in my stomach and starts to glitter there,
and words for happiness and freedom make
my skull ring like a bell and my ribs shake.
And God knows who's the greatest satirist,
whose the cold anger and the whippy wrist,
who was afraid enough to show contempt,
yet curious in every new attempt,
proud enough to be angry and not weep,
and loud enough to laugh rather than sleep.
Satiric truth, epigrammatic wit,
secret weeping and a hard open hit
became one thing in Alexander Pope,
the gadfly with midget skipping-rope,
the wild firedrake trailing a wounded wing,
the scorpion dying of his own sting.
Caverns and grottoes raped him in the dark,
his rest a glitter, his whole mind a spark.
Can you awake a new satiric age
without some poet in a hermitage?
The only poet of the age of doubt,
Byron is too far gone to write about,
and the few stinging poets now alive
are wild bees in the rocks without a hive.
Auden has been too clever for too long,
the sirens have drowned Spender in their song,
and the old showman of this dying fair

Eliot has sucked fire out of the air,
and vanished into fire, that fire is gone,
and we have all been charred to skin and bone.
The miners cough and work their vein alone.
Prose can be strong and funny, but the rot
withers that worst, young novelists are not
as absolute as poets ought to be;
God knows what is human integrity.
It is to scrape at heaven and be just,
know the clear diamond in the dead dust,
write what is good not what is innocent,
praise reason but not live by argument,
dive after truth, know nature, fight pretence,
admit we live at one another's expense,
be barbarous, love God and human life,
live where the hawk lives, strike with the sun's knife.
You may be godlike and admired and wise,
if you are not the thing you satirize:
live how you like, only write well, and then
we shall read it, and may die happy men.
Live by a lamplight blacker than the blind,
peer out at night through peepholes at mankind,
use a distorted lens, stare in the sun,
then make your subject a distorted one,
Powell at prayer or Douglas-Home at whist,
and learn from God to be a satirist.
Turn on the racehorse gangs and the full heat,
maggots and John Gordon and reasty meat.
But if this sort of stuff should make you sick,
there are three kinds of privileged critic
of whose unreasoned rage you might be glad,
prisoners, and schoolchildren, and the mad.
What those tormented minds see by bat-light
sober satire should settle down to write,
brush reasons off, drive poetry away,
bring raw nightmares prancing out at midday,
tell spirit how it lies, call hope a whore,
purge my stomach with laughter and terror.

God so loved us he sent his only son.
In the name of the Spirit of God. Amen.
Complete darkness: traditional sanctity:
now it is nearly midnight in my eye.
Darkness. The smell of flowers. Christmas night.
I am frightened by sanctity and light.
Somewhere it is all starting again,
worse than a dream. Christmas starting again,
lamplight choking to twilight on my table
I am colder than Christ was in his stable.
The house-walls shiver and sweat in the back-street,
grimy town-halls repeat and repeat
what my mouth drops, what English cannot say,
pink motor-tyres of roses, Christmas day.
I am terrified by what is beginning.
Think of the light opened like a live thing
to suffer and to be murdered again,
and then to be broken to pieces again,
to be alive and in prison, again.
Good God, what is human sanctity?
It is the barren dawn on the blank sea.
It can be a birthplace of liberty.
Say Christ is born tonight: he will be free.
We are breeding young soldiers to murder him.
The old judges are taking benzedrine.
Surely to be human is terrible,
and to be just is only to be feeble.
What is mankind? What is justice?
I say it is liberty and peace.
All enterprises of nature and reason,
what has been done to us, and we have done.
Peace is bounded by the season of death,
and by the just because their life is faith:
and the words for Freedom are prophecies.
I do not know what my religion is.

Christ is free and may suffer and can die,
how will you say freedom is heavenly?
God is free, reason free, nature wild:
I say God's freedom is born in this child.
I am afraid of what is beginning.
Darkness is not a liberating thing.
Christ is peace, reason, freedom, light,
I am the third world of the Queen of Night,
*Il Mondo*, with the moon on her forehead,
the dead language of words to wake the dead.
Christ will speak and his voice will be deep,
the stars will be ripe and the scythemen will reap,
the ground is opening in the field of sleep.
I am afraid of what is beginning.
And am humiliated by speaking.
God has silenced the four great winds in the sky;
outside my room the first traffic goes by,
hard beams of light are softening the roadside;
today it seems that God is without pride.
So much prison, such years of prison life;
we wake cold and anxious as a wet leaf;
we are in prison or break out of it,
on the road when only a few houses are lit,
or sleep tasting prison bread in our mouths
and all our working clothes are prison clothes.
In the moisture and mist a bird or two
bubble like watersprings, they come and go;
thirty years prison overshadow my mind,
I think England is prison of a kind,
and in that prison I am the blank wall,
the bare dark woods, the wind, this festival.
I am the one thing with no sap in it,
I am the dead wood, the prison habit;
I do not know how a tree can grow there;
I think Christ is that tree in midwinter:
eats raw field earth, is what a tree can be,
as tall and strong as a brick-works chimney,

and honourably wreathed round with green leaf,
and blessed and blessing heaven with green leaf.
I am terrified by such power to live;
mine is a life that can never revive,
I cannot stop nature and nature's course,
freedom is my idea of moral force;
good God, I do not know how to be free.
I know the axes are cracking for me,
and heavy saws are hissing in the dead wood.
Escaped prisoners cannot find their road.
The life of Christ is a kind of river,
cold, earthy water, nothing can live there,
I could live in it like a bird or fish,
a kind of season is my only wish.
So the white swan spoke in his cold love-nest,
the meditative, silent bird, at rest.
I do not know how I can live like Christ;
it is this world's profit and interest,
there is a profundity of language
and a disturbed goodness in this age.
I do not know how a man is profound,
after ten years I cannot understand
what it is like to live as Christ lived,
but am afraid of what I have believed.
The cock crows and the coloured crest retreats,
the plain-clothed policemen are in the streets
to clear a few drunken beggars away,
God said, *let there be quiet*. Christmas day.
Life is an agony of fear and noise,
there are handcuffs for hysterical boys.
It is a no man's land of tangled wires.
The dirtiest old men spit in their fires.
O great God, what is human life like?
The cracking of the rocks when the dead wake.
It is the haggard horses of the moon,
it is the smooth-haired horses of the sun.
But say the truth. What is human life like?
It is my vision when I am awake,

it is its own kind of reality.
The picture of Christ's nativity:
it seems too terrible to come true,
daylight consumed away by gold and blue,
the virgin deeper coloured than the star,
the winged creatures where peace and justice are.
The need to be silent in such a place.
The moon hides her equivocal face.
This mountain shivering with brute desire,
moist humanity in the hands of fire,
the sprig of greenery which the girl is:
the green grape in the arms of black branches.
I say the axe is banging in the trees.
I cannot comprehend these images,
there is always something left out of them,
a poetic justice I must condemn;
I see the river consuming the rock,
the lopped-off branches and the swishing hook:
and become free in a way thinking this.
I accept Christ and his calamities.
I see that he could not live to be old;
only disciples needed to be told;
Christ's freedom is a headlong moral force,
God lives, Christ speaks and nature takes its course.
What would it be then to know what Christ knows?
Theology is a mass of shadows,
nor was it in scholarly discipline
that what Christ has said had its origin:
it was in his untamed simplicity,
it was what God is and what I can be.
Break words open like breaking virgin ground,
God, man and nature will become profound
in your words and profound in your mouth:
break yourself up, what breaks you up is truth.
What makes a man profound is liberty,
Christ's life is an untamed simplicity.
I do not understand my religion;
I am always climbing back into prison.

I think I may be the new Frankenstein,
in my own street, shivering and coughing.
What Christ knows is an elementary thing,
and Christ's tragedy is the Iliad:
Homer is Christ, and the honours Christ had
are horse music, a small Balkan epic
that will make birds drop dead and the sky crack.
Everywhere it is snowing on the dead:
look how the glittering cover has been spread
over the blackened complicated dead
where the mist and the winter sun waded;
and it is snowing, it muffles the air,
the sun disappears in a blast of fire,
*Where are you God?* in the rustic desert,
I am freezing, these animals are hurt,
the white blanket of snow falls on and on:
I do not comprehend my religion.
I think it is a matter of cities,
as if I did not know what this street is
but was in love with its stone and darkness,
and have been wandering with no address
and am diminished. Christmas is mute.
Christ is reason and I am destitute.
I know what Christ knows. I know what God is.
Life is a dark process with no stages,
a decadence in which we confront God;
I tell myself that virtue is this road.
We are fractionally taller than the gods
who are lost now among the snowy woods.
I ask again what is human virtue?
I have believed that the gospel is true.
Now there is no way through this rough country,
but to become the mountain secretly.
The most merciful needs the most mercy.
Darkness, wrapping you round like a street light,
it wraps your body in the cloth of night.
Happy are the clear-hearted. They see God.
The war-blasted trumpet shall make them glad.

We are in heaven tonight in a way
and the dusty-throated organ will play,
God knows for Jack and Jill to get their wish
is *caritas et amor* in English.
Sometimes there is whisky and Christmas plays:
*I will appear here without a disguise,*
*my head is bare and my blood is darkness.*
That is what Death said to Love-in-idleness.
Sweet heaven, what is Christ, what is his love?
Life is his language and death is his proof.
I do not understand the world enough,
I was never master of my own roof,
I was born less than half an honest man,
and I am sure it would take a whole one
honest and Christ's equal to understand
how honestly Christ has loved mankind.
It is too simple and too powerful
a word, it has too vigorous a pull.
Soon it will be midnight of Christmas night.
I cannot say that love is the world's light,
I say Christ is elemental justice,
too clear to be light, too strong to be peace.
Murder will melt the crown on its own head,
Christ's words will end the world murder started.
I say Christ's justice is our undoing.
I dare not pray for the second coming.
God is free, Christ lives and will live freely:
I do not know what freedom will make me.
All through autumn, that colour and that cold,
I have beaten my brains to take some hold
on what the love and freedom of Christ does;
the bread that I eat in this place is his.
I think he is what the growing grain was
under the soaking North Oxfordshire earth,
in the absence of words, coming to birth.
I think God is the purpose of reason,
and is most silent when he is most known.

I cannot pretend to enlightenment,
God is a kind of unenlightenment,
I would not have said I had a soul,
I see the dawn breaking and the snow fall
and red and green lights flashing from Bristol.
Christ without God is an untrue defence,
divine praises are a false innocence,
I am in this darkness; my origin
is that Christ was born from a pure virgin.
We have been destroyed by God's liberty:
it seems to me that the sea and the sky,
the unreasonable, variable sea,
clouds, storms, mist, coloured immensity
make me a mirror of my universe,
and its weather is always growing worse.
A few seagulls fly crying in the sun.
When Christ comes and is in the air alone
over the sea-spray and green winter sea,
what is original justice to me?
Human hope. There are so many defeats.
I am frightened to see tanks in the streets.
Take an unsteady schoolboy, his whole sense
is an unskilful posture of defence;
I have ripened in the decay of time,
unskilfulness is always the same crime.
Christmas night. Christ meant what he said.
The swan swimming alone on his cold bed
paragon of cold snow-feathered whiteness
lives by the black river, but I do less.
Only that I am always at peace.
Despair is not in human intentions.
Roses open or die by their reasons.
I have believed sometimes I live by faith;
God knows if I shall be afraid of death.
The night of Christ's first animal breath
and the judgement day of his dying grief
are what I have most thought of in my life,

I do not know if I understand him.
I cannot be what is at war with time;
mysterious island of liberty
I say it is not covered by the sea,
good God, I cannot live my life, and now
I believe that the dead trumpets shall blow
*veritas, caritas* and we shall know
that the justice of God is Christ's virtue.
I have believed that the gospel is true.

## 155    Sermon on St Thomas More

We have not built the city of wisdom:
the ghost of God is what we started from;
and now the spirit of God is a dark wind
breaking the walls, and pentecost is blind,
the descent of the spirit is in blind fire:
we have not built the wisdom of God here.
Wisdom: the Word which was in the beginning
and is in God as it has always been.
God speaks to every generation:
the wisdom of God is not in London,
and yet the mouth of God opens in it,
the word of God is a human habit,
as common and enduring as the park grass:
it shakes the hand holding the whisky glass,
it can hang like spectacles on old eyes,
God broods in the infected silences.
We do not hear the wisdom of God well:
death is the clapper, terror is the bell
that speak most noisily in our belief,
but wisdom's words truly express life:
it is in the situation of love,
that is the city I am thinking of.
And what is coming now is the harvest
of lack of love, the increase of darkness.

Avalanches, breaking up of the ice,
falls of rock, fractures of the snow face
announce the new London, the world to come
that will not be the city of wisdom.
The word of God is not easily known,
it builds like bees in deserts and alone
cities of stone watered with holiness
the city where what should be is what is:
it is that one word which all time repeats,
whose children grow like fresh wheat in the streets;
the word of God is the word of reason,
which human nature and skill are founded on.
Little children, love one another:
hate avarice: let your justice appear:
this world withers: fear the future God:
the gospel is lived but not understood.


Think how Thomas More lived in this place,
think of that bookish, that sand-blasted face:
that life so heaven-loving, so death-fated,
the example too strong to be imitated,
the simplest and greatest of Englishmen.
Wisdom is justified in its children.
Truth is scribbled on water, it breaks like bone,
what Thomas suffered is written in stone.
His wisdom was not in earthquake and fire,
it was like the persistent, whistling air.
Thomas loved truth, not dragged it by the hair,
he said variety of opinion
would be of one mind in the world to come.


Later in time it is too dark to build
and the mind is far darker than the world.
What constitutes the darkness of this age?
It is barbarously cold, sharply savage,
obsessed with the memory of a dead God.
The gospel has never been understood.

Justice is a man rising from his grave.
Wisdom is God, the future God will save
the bricks and the ashes of this city,
God does not exist in the memory.
I know one day the voice of God will speak
louder and clearer than lightning can strike;
I do not know if God is patient
but I do know and fear he is present.
It is always the time of martyrdom,
and the moment for justice and wisdom.
God in his voice and in his word insists:
you are the Church of the faithful of Christ.
Where was it the pentecostal fire fell?
Was it on seven hills or on one hill?
Was it Rome, was it England it fell on?
It is the spiritual hill Sion.
And I say we have seen and shall see
the spirit like a fire in this city,
in which Christ's body and bread are broken
his words repeated and his blood given.
When will the city of wise love be built?
In the ruins of avarice and guilt
the justice of God will grow like fresh grass:
can it be the thirst of Christ on his cross
was an untamed love of the human race?
Christ's thirst has built the city of wise love,
whoever believes God's wisdom shall live.
This is the wisdom that Thomas died for:
it is a faith only God can restore.
There is always a Christ, always a cross,
always the city God will build in us.
And when the dead rise at the crack of doom
London shall be the city of wisdom.

Wisdom is building herself a house,
folly and avarice are out of use,
Christ's thirst has built the city of wise love:
the words are bread, you can eat them and live.

It is common to live by this belief,
wisdom is water and it revives life.
Life is the spirit of Christ in the creed
and the cold water from his dying side.
All wisdom is in God and it has been
in God from before the beginning.
Wisdom marks the chosen people of God:
it is the spirit: it is true and good.
We have been marked by God with holiness:
God's chosen people is the human race.
For God's sake let us study Christ's mercy;
the body of love can be this city,
its soul is spiritual liberty.
Liberty is mankind's oldest friend,
it is the knowledge of God in the end.
The inheritance of God's children shall be
liberty: equality: fraternity.

Thomas More in his words and his living
was a man obedient to the king,
and his whole family in his presence
showed gentle manners and obedience:
his reason was free, God was his confidence.
He was Cato: he would not compromise;
terrible honesty sat in his eyes.
God's spirit descended on his prison
like a dark pentecost to his reason.
Heavenly wisdom the last thirst of Christ
human sorrow's acid and analyst
gave him knowledge of God, freedom of mind,
true lover and true brother of mankind.

Wisdom is a city and the spirit
of Christ in his last hour is building it,
the tower of his last breath still soars up
over the broken bread, the given cup,
and to recall it, to speak it again
is new life and religion of all men.

The river of wisdom in this city
runs from a rock the people cannot see:
London has lived with unwisdom so long,
we are all fugitives from that chain gang,
unreason, avarice, lack of delight,
unbrotherhood, unliberty, unlight.
Christ in his death spoke the first words of life,
there is no other bedrock of belief,
we believe and enact his death and love,
this is a reasoning nothing can move,
this is the city of heaven's graces
where the children are as tall as the trees:
nothing can live in it but what is pure
and what is without fear, and will endure;
what we look for is what we started from,
God is the city, love is the wisdom.

## 156   Whitsunday Sermon

*Apposuit tibi aquam et ignem.*
God's breath and spirit entered into them,
they were sprinkled with the water of life:
Abraham is my father in belief,
Peter is my father in the spirit:
I have been sprinkled and can speak by it.
The descent of the spirit was tongues of fire
each hanging separately in the air.
The word and spirit of God entered them.
*Apposuit tibi aquam et ignem.*
These are words of victory and of peace:
Christ is in our people and will increase,
true, divine society cannot cease.
This feast of prophecy has no meaning,
my brotherly words are an empty thing,
they are a beating on doors, shouts for light,
unless it is true God sent his spirit

to illustrate the last ages of time.
I say he never dies. God is my dream,
but the dream is a false, future belief,
it is young Buddha on his lotus leaf:
what I fear is the Christ who is coming,
his tongues of fire, his spirit descending.
He has set fire and water before me.
They say Christ is primal history.
The spirit comes like water and like fire
and sibilates prophecies in the air;
the idea of God is a mountain of ice,
there is nothing so merciful as justice,
yet the heaven of justice cannot fit
the rainfall and the fire of the spirit:
drops of water and fire: do not fear them:
*apposuit tibi aquam et ignem.*
We have waited for the first words of God,
they are a language we have understood;
in the first world of time, in the pure age
God created man naked in his image;
we have all confusedly understood
what are life, death, evil and good.
History now is human enslavement;
God is leading the slaves out, God went
to the desert in the second world of time:
the mountain of fire Moses could not climb,
and the column of water at midday,
I mean the Law, the Word Moses could say,
this water and this fire in the desert
lead the slaves into that sand which is our part.
We are baptized by the thing we desire,
in the sea-passage, in the hill of fire.
The spirit and the breath of God are free,
God is not tolerant of slavery;
and now God is leading the slaves out:
beloved, Christ is the ram which was put
into the bush for Abraham's son,
the freedom Christ teaches murders no one.

When God powerfully entered those men
the tongues of fire were wise language, doctrine:
the spirit and the word were at one then.
When God shall lead an enslaved people out
the anger of God comes to town no doubt:
suns run down, mountains of rock hide their head,
there are separations of living and dead.
But God's word and spirit has entered us,
Christ is in our people and will increase:
these are words of victory and of peace.
I do not know if the spirit can live
in something so weak and so fugitive
as the confused consciences of these times,
but I do know that the whole earth in flames
is not that fire which God sets before me.
The world's new age is slave society,
and God knows until we are free of it
no one can speak the words of the spirit.
The spirit now is as dumb as a dove
dropping mere water in the mouth of love.
*Apposuit tibi aquam et ignem.*
Our love and our duty interpret them
as all baptisms we were baptized with:
the last Christian baptism is death.
Christ's dying language says we were baptized
in icy water in the death of Christ
when the new Eve was ripped out of his side
and he knew her and spoke as Adam did.
And we shall be baptized in our own death:
our first true language is a dying breath:
what this baptism expresses is life,
the breath and tongue of God work in belief.
You say God, and it means nothing at all,
but the same mist will close in on you all,
the stars and planets are fireworks that fall.
*Apposuit tibi.* It tolls for thee.
Death made Christ sweat for his victory.

Visitations of God in death happen.
God in his trumpet raises up dead men,
God in his spirit and wise proceeding
in the breath of his mouth and trumpeting
shall proclaim freedom and life to all men,
the sea shall vomit and the earth open,
the dead shall be raised like Adam, naked,
first in paradise when there were no dead.
The fire and water of God is spirit:
learn to speak in the language of light.
Fire burns the wheat, rain engenders the wheat.
The spirit of God is still prophetic,
there is no society we can make
God cannot break down again brick by brick.
This inspiration that sets free slaves
and whatever God's free spirit achieves
are by God but not God, God is free,
inspiration is not epiphany,
God freely encountered and understood
is the epiphany and love of God,
there is no epiphany of the spirit
but water, fire and the language of light,
and the gospel which is written in it.
What is true, good and merciful in this age
batters to bits in the big mill of language,
the spirit is dove-music, tongues in the air,
and mere reseparated tongues of fire:
but is spirit: there is God when all's done,
I fear and recognize his heavy tone.
The riddles of wisdom are a nightingale.
We know Christ in his last evening meal.
We hear God's words before he has said them.
*Apposuit tibi aquam et ignem.*
I cannot say the spirit speaks in me,
but I can know and say that I am free
by God and by his spirit and breathing,
and that the law of God is life-giving.

Here is a mystery. Our belief is
when God breathed on the face of brute darkness
there was created light, and in Moses
God gave the law, which law shall be and is:
and the law is the word, the word is Christ,
and his speaking and spirit have not ceased,
in the twelve, in privacy, in their room,
in the church, in many voices, in Rome.
The spirit is free, also he makes free,
an apple reddens better in its own tree,
we know only that the spirit can move
in many branches like the voice of love.
We shall be baptized by death into life,
and by the awful notes of human grief,
by what is done to me, by what I am;
my soul is drenched in the death of Adam.
God in the room, in the twelve, in spirit
commanded such words of effective light
that they expressed nature unfalsified;
the spirit speaks humanly, Christ died.
And like pure sand, in spirit dying men
suffer Christ's death again and again;
the fire of Christ and the water of Christ,
in which on this day we have been baptized,
by the good spirit which Christ understood
as freedom raising up children to God.

When Eliot died it made him seem human,
nineteen sixty five has been
one hoarse tap tap tap of a black stick,
black water dripping on a dead train.

I never had a dream so powerful
as when Eliot died. He pulled this year
like a black car over a dead moor
in a blue mist, through words and things of fear.

When he died I went into real mourning,
poems are wrecked, this is the sea-bottom:
the anchor-chains of reason drag and swing
backwards and forwards with a squeak like doom.

Now say seven hundred years ago
Dante died: heavenly innocence
like a wild bush of roses cannot grow.
and the starving forest has broken its fence.

Since his time nature is ingrowing;
thinking of Dante what I wonder most
is when the inferno like a complete dream
will eat my poems and swallow my ghost.

No one has spoken as clearly as they did
or in such austere words of poetry:
the angel of language is visible,
the fire stands in the air over the tree.

Heaven is intellectual, to feel
at home there goes beyond man and woman:
and I have never dreamed of such a thing.
When Eliot died, it made him seem human.

*quomodo sedet sola civitas*


The belly of death has trumpeted.
The last word of Christ has been said.
He is inside the houses of the dead.
He suffers on this night and every night
and always alone in his father's sight:
he is mankind, justice crucified,
and modern history is how he died,
and the trees have black buds like iron pins,
his wound is running, our decline begins.
God is in the blue heavens looking down,
he sees the shadow of the English crown,
the destroyed city, idle metal, fire,
the destitute defrauded of his hire,
wolf-packs, the iron blot and the blood-blot
and the free voices where freedom is not.
Mankind is Christ, and he shall agonize
even when the blood dreams. It never dies.
Cloth and wood, plaster and brick, this town
is cracking, shattering and rumbling down
because the dying Christ hangs down his head:
happy are the unborn and the sainted.
And the mountain of God is ruined rocks
and the angels of death have reaping-hooks.

The beginning of the world, the breath of God,
will be the last thing to be understood:
at this time the one blessing God can bless
is justice, crucifixion, holiness.
The mountain of God is in the just
and Christ will blossom in those rocks and dust.
He is the long good habit of mankind,
the unknown familiar, the never friend.

There is nothing better than to be free,
there is nothing decent except sanctity.
Human hope and an old self-interest
bend mankind back into the shape of Christ,
from suffering and death comes reasoning,
Christ is reason from this planet's beginning.
Reason is Christ: by faith is by his death
and the dark tower of his dying breath,
and this darkness has the texture of ice,
it is the stubborn freezing of justice:
it is the freshness of the death of men,
the newness of the one or of the ten:
on the rooftops, in prisons, in the street,
and the archangel in the dying wheat.
I know that it will never be finished,
and nothing but Christ is fit to be wished.

But if the truth is inbuilt in reason
God has suffered for the death of his son.
I have no way to understand love,
or what the spirit of God is made of,
only the dreadful moaning of his wings
disturbs the dark of my imaginings,
and in the father's sight his son dying
is worse than Good Friday's most lasting spring.
Yet we can never really forget
the last vision Christ had of this planet:
the judgement we must fear is that moment,
mercy is earthly, justice heaven-sent.
The forgiveness of God spoke in his death
and the slow gasping of his painful breath.
Mercy is Christlike, Christ has christened it,
faith wakes at midnight walking by it,
it is the one rock that shall never split.
The forgiveness of God is the darkest pit.
In that darkness of love our groanings start,
the length of life, the feebleness of art,

the unearthly comets of true love, the wild
blushings of fire as lovely as a child:
the salt springs of love are on Calvary
and the cross where Christ died is Adam's tree.
Human love has a wooden death-bed,
and justice on earth ends as Christ ended:
it is a crying out to God in faith,
it will blossom again out of its death.
I say the just shall not be deserted,
they shall not be confined among the dead,
and when the justice of God shall break out
they shall be fire, and their spirits will shout
in the sun at midday in the blue air,
walking with snow feet and with starlight hair,
God and man shall believe them, and each one
will speak, and what they say shall be done.
Many shall be in glory at that time
who are lost in the dark of obscure time:
they shall find words for Christ, his dying eye,
the worst and the best good in history.

I am rotten wood, there is no fruit in me,
Christ is the only fruit on Adam's tree.
And I wander in a dark wood of trees,
the fruit of Adam's tree is mysteries:
wounded flowers, fruit living and dead,
the fruit is blushing, the blossom is red.
I know who I am, I am not what I am.
I will eat the fruit of the tree of Adam.
There is no fruit so red or so white,
it is as plain as water and as light,
no thorn is so sharp, no honey so sweet,
the bread of death, which is the living wheat.
Who can bear God or his forgiveness?
Only this fruit is blessed and can bless.
It is reason and the world is darkness.

I am not able to say in God's eyes
that Christ always suffers or lives or dies;
the murder of the just men continues,
that is a Christ no language can confuse.
God's kingdom and justice are a prison:
I say Christ is light, freedom, reason.
In the island of pains and of gains
the English angel is weeping in chains.
In the island of the justice of God
the sufferings of Christ are understood:
the weeping of the just man is lucid,
mine was confused, I wept for what I did.
The sufferings of Christ are understood:
*Thus be these good yeomen gone to the wood*
*as light as the leaf is on the lime tree.*
Merciful God, give such lightness to me.
Christ has had his agony in England,
which was the green and is the promised land,
we can never again repair that loss
but by nailing ourselves to the same cross,
love being simple, justice being plain,
and Christ's birth coming again and again.

All movement goes into a state of rest,
labour into tranquillity, the best
of wisdom moves into the loveliest.
Christ rested in an earthly grave.
What I most love is what I have.
Abundance is given, it springs, is not priced,
blood and water out of the side of Christ
have bloodied my thoughts and watered my life,
with a green freshness like the tree of life,
and the freshness of justice is in leaf.
The wild cherry increases, the grape dies,
there are seasons even of centuries:
and of murders and sufferings and lies.
The prison is the street: the lonely farm
will not be broken open without harm:

the dirty flag degrades the uniform.
And all this suffering will increase
until the anger of reason makes it cease.
*Vox populi ira Dei,*
voice of the people wrath of God, say I.

And on this day Christ died.
It was for love and was his only pride:
it was the rock he struck and travelled to,
on this day he did what he meant to do.
It was the wrath and whisper of the dove:
the pure and original spring of love.
And all this suffering will increase,
the tree of Christ is the tree of peace,
and quietly and harshly the spirit
is breathing, speaking, weeping into it,
he drops like a dewfall into the breast,
he is the true poison, the fruit, the rest,
he is the victorious wind of life,
and voice of the brackish river of grief:
his nest is pure, and his wing is justice,
the tree of Christ is the tree of peace.
Human right shall be God's right hand and throne,
God is spirit, and one, and one alone.

Justice shall be like the snow and the sea.
Christ is the end of all calamity,
and what is true and strong shall come to birth.
There shall be no more wickedness on earth.

## 159  Canticum

*for John and Anya Berger*

*Adde poemata nunc, hoc est, oleum adde camino,*
*quae siquis sanus fecit, sanus facis et tu.*


1

Not to fear madness.
Scattered with sunlight out of doors or in
with a cat on my knee, a homely craze
and instruments of music never used,
no prayer meetings, a smell of damp,
a God dispersed in lightnings.
I tell you there is thunder in the tree.


2

When the coal is dark.
Daybreak was red and grey, greyer than red.
You drink tea and the rivers of the mist in the street,
squeezing away the clover from your thought
and when the fire
is isolated then
summon the swan the nightingale the nightjar
liberated from their sound.
Now the lake you feared in a foreign city
is filled with waterbirds.
Liberated from these dreams and their meanings.
In the future they will not dress like us.

3

The future is the truth, another season
old people wreathed in roses when the pears are yellow
it sharpens and the wasp is drugged asleep.
Death is my atmosphere
it has walks and waters
where the head of the mountain always is.
And the loving, intoxicated trees
turn to stone in the water and breathe snow.
In the short afternoons people will come
and understand the future
and carry it homewards in their hands.


4

The weary sun of nineteen one vomited learned men
onto the new planet. Rocks were on fire.
But when the sun got younger it devised
prison cities of green and of blue glass.
Everything is past.
And in the future I shall grow apples
and hear the languages of birds.
The walnut trees are taller than the tower.
My grandfather was innocent trade.
My father's name is War.
The truth is in the street.
We will make this be true.
The children shall have apples.

5

The corrupt fox and the cold absent owl
are the worst citizens of a cloud island.
Rain traces them hopelessly through bushes.
What the rain loves it murders.
The place has troops of rain hunting like dogs
and the farm people are lost in the clouds.
The wet stone gives them twinges.
If there were music here
it would be old tunes hammered out
on dusty strings, it must be resistant.
The yellow bird, the vixen and the fox
have magnified their voice against the clouds.
Twenty miles off is another cloud island.


6

Mountains awestricken like alchemists.
The torn books have fermented.
Then rivers and branches run down to me.
And God has become young, has become just,
the Holy Ghost is locked up in a book,
and God is spitting natural fire.
The city drips to death like a candle.
No heavenly spirit shall prophesy
in the age to come;
we shall go out to squares in the evenings
with public fountains, light and spray,
but no one will remember history,
no one will remember us.

## 7

The tattered papers on the wall
used to instruct me once:
they hung around my chair like singing masters.
Now that the fire is cold
the light also less yellow
I try to warm them with my small blood but
the world is dead tracks that I never knew,
and how can I get back to the desert?
It is not much to ask.
You climb for days winding past threads of water
then everything is snow and then rock
and then sand with villages of poplars.
How can I get back to the birch forest
where God being so old
had become also the future?
The big white poppies will be harvested
higher than the mountains of India.
The future there
is hardly beginning to be born.
How hard it is to push through history.


## 8

To break out of this nature and to reach
the love-infected flocks of swans eating
the pure grain of religion.
Then lights shone
that make all cities
into the past. Their power is this:
it is always the same conversation,
if you die and I die, grow, go away
others will come here with the same wild faces,
wishing the same.
If you carried the city with your hands
in a labyrinth of ladders and smoke

you could break out saying the simple words
that destroy nature. Look,
there are no birds in the apples this year:
the tree is dead and only full of leaves.


9

Walk into death bring away the blossom,
it opens into field after field,
clover, hedge-parsley, lilacs, apple trees,
and the grey pigeon flying up in flocks.
We must take from it now,
every boy must be told
to rape in that meadow.
Shadow on grass is green but dusk-coloured.
Not one by one but everyone breaks in,
we shall come back with armfuls of lilac
and the crooked trees behind our kitchens
will blossom again. It is the future
which says death to us and which we love.


10

Now we are walking where it will be dark
lake trees hedges gulls one sheet of soot.
The puppet grimaces.
And I am troubled by light fantasies.
The coldness of the natural cycle
tears into rags of coldness at daybreak,
this is not natural: God made it so:
the green and white herb and the violin
with other auguries that I believe
unite in lamentation of spirit.
This for the dead
and the holy one, blessed be he.

11

A ring of guns like a stone monument.
This landscape will never be rid of it.
It is out of sight only as the dead are
on the edge of shallow hills.
In the small hours
sucking on iron like the pap of dark
you create wheat, clover, villages
sprouting from iron seed. The sun dazzles,
it smells of bracken fires and mist and bread.
Commit my spirit to the air and fire,
the owl-hoot not the starlit monument.


12

In the mist owlfire.
A thing of stone is burning in the mist.
Their time is not in minutes.
It crumbles language into ragged verses:
marshlights, candles, the innocent firefly
and everything that breathes or is still
has flames of fire.
The sun's clouded crest, the plover's cold crest,
green outer branches shaking on cold trees
set fire to my eyesight when I am cold.
The world heaves its shoulders
to carry rock and ice.
The smallest fire is fine ash in the heart.
A cold thing to survive.
To be free is now. To be strong is now.
Ice is coming, it has fire of a kind.

13

Madness is this.
It worms finely inward through ivory,
while the face and the lines on the face
engross the sun as if I were ploughed earth.
What is not noble cannot be insulted.
God disappearing in a flock of birds
at a gun-clap a mile over hedges
does not insult honest intelligence.
Spirit worms inward. Rain coming.
I see the future as the true season,
dense and bewildering, like snow.
There is a blankness that will draw it down.
Virtue is underground. It burrows inward,
engenders life, the roots of wintersweet.


14

The cow whale plunging through the green tumult
sniffs out her breeding water to lie still,
when snow candies the cliff.
And the thin Arctic swan over desert
tracked with frost-coloured horses on the ground,
worshipped with herbal fires, down to the green
poplars and the amazing tall weeds.
And the sun's hunt will never end. Is over.
When is the beginning of history?
The breeding-ground
is still, it is not here.
What fruit will grow here in the coming age?
Lichen and granite watered by the sea
the mollusc and the always turning surf
will be the treasure of the world to come.

## 15

Madness can build a city like a bird
in the thick brush of twigs, in the fresh leaf
and rocking breath of empty-minded heaven.
The city of jackdaws is not united
by written laws or musical hymns.
They live by breath, it scatters their future.
The mad city is united shadows,
bird-language in the forest of tall trees.
In the future city music will be
simpler than languages learnt in the woods,
and solemn laws will have their kind of music.
God will speak better English than now.
The old people created this language,
these words and cities like a shadow-play.

## 16

Sober feeling: to be decent in a chair.
Buds ripen in the mist one morning.
The night-smells of the tree
penetrate windows, bring the cold inside.
Consider to be silent fifty years,
a few words, a handful of humus.
Something was chalked up on a ragged wall,
the wall entranced it with the air and dark:
hero who cuts away the dragon-wing,
child of machinery in the darkness,
intoxicated by the breaths of daybreak,
words not written, which will be written.
Night after night I open my window
to remember the dawn sobriety,
to speak in language, to be instructed.

## 17

Past history is the sap of my words,
dawn after dawn and words after words,
the bare dead and the dewfall and the nightlamps.
The future town too heavy to balance,
pink lichen on white shells,
the ornamental plume, the waterbird:
justice is the river in the desert,
we were enslaved, broke rock for rivers,
river is breaking rock
at dawn at midday in the dusk at night,
rock cracks, it will not be stopped up.
The name of this water is foreign words,
the sweat of slaves and the dew in the earth
which was desert and is not. Is pure and runs.


## 18

The air starved in winter:
a mouth of branches and a bed of snow:
violet flashing at the edge of the wood.
One night we shall break through into that time.
Children will warm their hands in museums
running and whistling through the guarded rooms.
Time is a skeleton of giant bones
as white as salt, should not have seen sunlight.
And summer be like blossom in wartime,
thicker than it was fifty years ago.
The fruit-shadows on metal are to come,
the bone-structure of time in midwinter
foretells a flower of the age to come.
The bones of time and the meadows of snow
will blossom sooner when that flower comes.

## 19

Innocent music strays
among mad writing, winter afternoons,
but I know we shall never come back.
This is the weather of a future time
when muses ride their cycles in the crowd
and the earth smells sharply at the weekend.
In the street they are talking of local news.
In the London of the world of the dead,
utopias, all cities of the dead,
they read satiric writers for the words they use.
All this is past.
Russet and checkered geese in future time
will feed to monotonous flutes.
All these words will have crumbled in the people's speech.
And I have already forgotten my life,
and have forgotten.

1

A sandy rock, my one name crusted over,
and I do not remember my father's name.
Was scything widely in a league of grass
ten days with the long tongue in balance,
it will be sharp in the black of greenness.
I have trodden down flowers without names.
I shall invent, sweat, I shall not speak.
                                     Building in limestone
with a construction differs from a tree:
or when the airy clang may be in flight,
invisible, the stone will be breathing.
While my long scythe will bite and whistle in
the wizzened regiment, it falls in line.
                                     I shall begin
with the sky open morning and evening.


2

The horizon is green ink and blue ink,
and the trees inky colours,
except for the wild cherry which is white.
Then death is nothing, a dark edge:
but the spirit, the moral, the absurd?
It is an absolute of majesty.
Then love's a bed, purple and white and grass,
no star so purple and a water-shoot.
Who can believe in the God of nature?
Is nothing, nothing, a dark edge:
it hangs in the air like a smell of snow.
And reading in the book's memory I
can prophesy pages by pages
and can labour in the words of a song,
and can begin.

### 3

Who thought deeply, loved also what was living.
Virtue was in the mountains, in the stony villages,
magpie in meadow,
swiftly the shade, swiftly the afternoon.
The shepherd sees the city it is in his eye.
The oracle is water. Stone shall prophesy.
I am lost in this deserted extent.
Eagle his eye so brilliant in air
he will consume away the shepherd's eye.
There is succession of times in God,
but my identity is seasonal:
aspires, is blood and feathers, mows mid-air,
nor do I live for what is living,
I am frightened to awaken those who sleep,
or brush their eyes with nameless flowers.
In sleep the soul recovers its nature.
But virtue is in the mountains, in the stony villages.


### 4

So black as is midnight.
So strong as is the wind.
You hear the creaking of the iron gate
seeming to move on mountains,
the moon stone-footed in the sun's eclipse,
hopeful of green and white. You will go back,
eat honey in darkness, tread down clover,
lie in cress and in grass.
Today there is no moral only mountain wind,
tomorrow's snowy outline will visit
the air as lightly, in sleep as lightly.
It is the ruins, you will live in them.

5

Should have been what the dark is
and imitate fruit trees extend shadows.
Turkish roses sweated in shadow.
Chill and wet in my grandfather's linen
I see trees and woods how they extend.
The knocking of the axes of daylight.
Chill and wet in the leather on my feet.
Poor as a pebble. Stars were foreign armies,
they never whistled morning or night-watch.
I do expect that motion like a star
was once familiar to the darkness.
Now should be dark
and should extend in the grain of a tree,
but that my mouth and hands are like a star.
Poor as a pebble.


6

On this rock the fineness of ivy
painted with suns or shadows
and valleys, airs, the coarsest lavender.
Wordless, and to begin again.
Iris, anemone, long grass:
what has been lost is never in nature,
it is not to be found by the snow-horses
that I can hear in the bones of my head
nor in the absolute difference of the sea.
At night this bone is frozen,
they scatter frost and ice,
champing the glitter of fragments and the mist.
Outside, uncovered, in the wind and mist.
The dead trumpet was shrieking, it has blackened.
Grief is the principal leavings of time.

*May–December* 1971

219

Rain was down and the dark broke open.
An ageing bird his face an ageing man
in the twenty coloured moments of dawn:
a bushy herb, the stone sides of the mountain.

White hair, with vision in his ear and eye:
prophets on horses winding from the sea,
over the black rock and the yellow sea-spoil,
the prophecies drained up into the sky.

He sees these flowers of the coming time,
tongued with a wooden root full of fresh leaf,
the sea-wind whistles one self-loving tune,
the words and feet of prophets carry life.

The shivering bird's body has three wings,
one winnows in heaven never bending,
one sweeps the earth sweating on everything,
the third wing searches round him and between.

What he sees, what he hears is not music,
brick by brick walls of water will break
and mental roses wither on the spike,
prophets go barefoot on the sand and rock.

He shall reign king for a year in the mountain,
all curtains of colours will flutter down,
virgins will drink from the springs again:
an ageing man, his face an ageing bird.

**162**   *for Miranda again*

In love expecting to be disappointed:
violet, white, carnation.
And yesterday the fog
last ragged heads, chink chink of a bird,
then one white tablet into clear water.
Love's delirious unlimited theme.
It is the conversation of darkness
which you have listened to fifteen years.
What is light, fresh and peaceful?
Heaven of sleep on a pillow of time,
among the lemon trees and the white chickens.
Frog in the well. Cresses in the streams.
Dreams are in colours, in a few words.
And the God of my family in the dream.


**163**


The future writings of a hand of stone:
star-white and ragged in the mossy crumble
this residue of reason time will not exhaust,
and residues of nature reason will exhaust:
the sky's marbled end-paper, the moon's green taper,
stone and woods in the unexhausted mouth.
There is no architecture at that time,
love is a prejudice of small-nosed animals,
flowers in tongues of colours in the April turf.
It is the undertow of the motionless moon-driven surf;
it is the architecture of that time
and future writings of a hand of stone.

The seagull's wing: snowfall of the fog:
dark drizzles on the dead window,
time has spread out like ink in quarter-chimes.
In the writing up of human history
I sense a tragical beat:
snowfall is the balance of the universe,
black-pupilled Venus will be glittering
over the simple pleasures and the simple sleep.
Eternity is thin and unmixed
against the candy of these small, sensory bones.

The breath which is crystalline is obscure,
and the green bark, the purity of the air,
and the raincloud head downwards in the flood
and the animal pelt of the bushes and reeds
wait for a late bird roaring in the yellow dregs.

It is hard to conceive this,
to oppose green virtues to the withering away of breath,
the still unreaped planet and the mineral fire
of suns like dews to snowy conviction.

The age dropping like snow
onto the unripe faces of our history.

**165**

In the damp the new stems,
in the black the bare trees,
in the white light yellow-eyed the moon
the ivy streaming on the tree,
the darkness under the crust
could break and drown the globe;
it would be black and green.


**166**     **Shakespeare's Birthday**

Gum-scent is two days, then it disperses
to clouds of leaf in mid-air, a green stain
is in grey air and will be in the blue air
fresh cantonment of shadows for conversation,
hungry for verse and music being thin.
When garden sciences inoculated
simple roses they had been weak and small,
the muskrose doubled, no one can go back.
O draggled hedges or stringed instruments
and mothers of nine muses, memories,
countries that future time abolishes.
The string is singing, the season the same,
the leaf is simple, the air is as cold.

## 167

Deserted rooms all giving onto this:
the night bare-footed, the hours night,
a breath of frost, whiffs of river and reed,
black leaf, the musk of mere earth,
the unripe piping, the sun ascending.

What died ripe and has become this?
What never lived is wild and ripe enough
and love is an unfinished process,
like the ripe cold, the moment of morning.
It finishes. The sun is ascending.


## 168

Honeysuckle is breaking down the wall,
the garden is abandoned,
water is coming brown out of the taps,
the wooden ruins of the cycle shed
house a sewing-machine and a swede-chopper.
I have no wish to communicate
with the past of old iron and darkness.
I am moved by relics. The walls are cracked.
I could live in such a house,
and in the end I will. It will be decent
to end with nothing, my kind of nothing.
You could entertain your last friend in it,
you could avoid the district visitor,
burn fires on the damp hearth, keep a chicken,
cough, be rheumatic, drink brandy.
The blackbird is my priest.
The soot-smell is the incense of daybreak.
I could buy a tea-pot, grow a beard
and become what no one can put in words.

# 169    Pigs

*(for Deirdre)*

I

They survive,
so did Dick Wernham,
in 1948 like a jockey to look at,
he liked to live near them.
He had ten pigs and a pensioned off horse,
and one heroic sow,
moon-backed, hairy-backed, heavy,
she smelt sweet and she used to kiss him.
The roads smelt of tar and leaves,
she was the nearest pig to Westminster,
you didn't hear that roar of the traffic,
she broke out and adventured in fields,
and the horse broke out,
unshod and feathertufted,
the police always brought her back.
It must have broken Dick Wernham's heart
when they put down his pigs.
He went where there were others.
In forests where there were truffles
there must have been concentrations of pigs.
A sea of moons in the black undergrowth.
Tusk bristle, muscle
in the enormous gloom
and sows like white sandbanks
rooting and snooting.
The steady fall of acorns in the middle ages.
Menalcas dirty with the mush.
Dick Wernham near the bypass.
They like clean food.
They like clean straw.

You see them among thistles and loosestrife.
They have bad tempers.
Pigs are my heroes.
They survive.


2

Pigs refuse pork sausages
coated in chocolate. They do sniff them.
Sows murder piglets.
What has some smell of incest
is not sheer cold horror.
Who write this, an old silver-bristle.
I am brutish enough.
They are brutish enough.


3

Warm-blooded, they can work up heat
lying closely together.
The prickly warmth of straw like a nest.
This in captivity.
Wild they wallow in body-size craters
but not together. Space is freedom.
Humans are tender-skinned,
touch on green fleeces of grass,
must be together clasping with fingers.
Strip them, they feel absolutely naked.
If we lived wild it would be otherwise,
harsh stubble, impenetrable skins.


4

But eating is in this relationship.
The flavours of pork, curing of ham.

And I admire the apricot-fed man.
It is all in this: his running, his snorting,
the chequered French light in the forest,
the heavy jungle light blasting the mist,
pathetic understanding of senses
not built to understand.
I see them run,
sniff them at home. I am an animal,
my spirit is what says I sniff the pig.
I am in the forest with the pig.


5


They will not take snowfall.
They pelt down from the mountains under snow,
to shelter in coniferous forest.
They dislike wind.
They are in deciduous woods without leaves
rooting in deep bracken
gone before the first violet,
meanwhile they are victims of guns,
men with dogs shouting in the level light,
lonely duckshooters and deerstalkers
stand hissing in their tracks.
They are blue sides and bristles as the trees
might be if they could run and feed,
refugees from the astounding white and blue,
disgruntled in a cloudburst,
they steam like clouds and sleep at night.
By lakes in woods the yellow brown and black
shattered by hunters in the afternoon
are undisturbed at dawn.
They go by at dawn.
A bang and smoke. Squealing and blood.
Churned mud. The boars deeper in forest.
Another dawn, another lakeside.
Fatally further from the rock and ice.

The green shoots of bushes.
They run in spring, follow water upstream.
In summer in the highest tangles of trees,
no one can ever track them at that time,
whole families run wild with no fear.


6


Pigs in a story behave in the story
like pieces of a crystal universe.
History is opaque and various.
The languages of pigs are intimate
and mostly in proverbs.
There is no word for the stalk of cabbage,
and the fox has none for the smell of kale.
Pigs hardly understand their own language,
and have no word 'happy' or 'universe'.
They are not stylish in their performance.
Their styles are many absences of style.
Pigs in a story accept the story.
In life they accept life.
Their life is dense and has changes
which are not absent in the world of man,
and the delusions of pigs are minimal,
their consolation cold and crude.
Landscape with pigs:
they have their religion:
it is to eat and to survive.
They smash gardens, ignore statues
and straggle through sunsets like streams.
They like leisure.
They amuse Greeks but Romans are afraid,
the gospel is no place for a pig.
They amble among marginal drawings.
They are earthy, they own the underworld.

**7**

I grieve for the big pigs of prehistory,
the blue-spotted, the long-backed,
the solid works of man:
enormous in their field one morning,
shaming an artist, dwarfing a sty,
treasured by a farmer in a flat hat
within sound of the shooting in the wood.
All that has lived is the piggy eyes of squires
and the long backs of acorn-fed women.

**8**

Rooting in her meadow she looks happy.
Life has chosen her.
She stands at the centre of a big world,
extensive in time and in distance.
Dandelions grow under the hedge.
River, wind, bucket compete
in the background of music.
Something complete about her
shows in her tilt and her gesture.
Her size in her proportion
is queenly and her shadow majestic,
her children agile, naked and well fed.
No one can tell you if she understands
the difference of grasses, taste of nettle,
texture and smell of undersoils.
She is a good farmer:
slow, ruinous, productive,
breathing by the advantages of tax,
she likes the light and the climate,
gargantuan in winter in the river mist,
drunken among rotting apples under trees.

9

In human art the pig and the fish
unless you allow the Greenland whale
produce no masterworks. Fear that is
to see myself as pig or as fish?
What is given and will not alter.
It might be revelation in a dream:
dream well enough, then when you wake
you are still unable to describe a pig.
A small pig of bronze, a little work
to stand for the great herds of history.
A white pig in a green field.


10

Pigs went to the dead in Canaan.
The man is naked hollow alabaster,
holding a pig of hollow alabaster,
the pig's hoof on the man's balls,
the man's hand on the pig's balls,
it was not solid but the wine ran
out of them both from the snout.
It was poured out like blood for the dead:
the wine came from them both.
Therefore in my religion
the prophets of God forbade pigs.

11

Pigs are the moon's creatures,
and the small hedgehog moving at night
and the grey and black badger in moonlight
are the English moon's priest and acolyte.
No one is left to worship the moon.
The woods are more abandoned than churches.
Pigs are the moon's people,
but now there is no goddess of the night.


12

Humans make bad pigs,
old silver-backs with rosy faces
clever with truffles, hating each other,
bristlers and tuskers upright in chairs
pleased with possession, liking their smell,
dark hairy snorters in undergrowth,
brushed Foreign Office pigs with swine eyes
and gloating piglets of great families.
They are the poor relations of true pigs,
they never get their snouts in real buckets.
They lack hedges and mist and cabbage-stalks.


13

If a pig had a philosophy
it would be like mine.
Random is necessary to a pig.
Pig-language is not random to a pig.
Homeric pigs are in the dark past:
they ripped Adonis, died by iron.
And all those ages have been lost.
And their best years were from Purcell to Bach.
They dimly remember the Shakespeare of pigs.

You run down sometimes, you go blind,
cobwebs of yellow paper in the trees,
damp weather, quietness of a kind,
olive, grape, there are no distances:
you fumble the world for touch and sight,
stone underfoot, animals, half-light.

And this is such a time now:
rain and flies and the end of something,
and you dressed for the worst weather and so
here comes the world you were imagining,
it is yellow and grey again outside,
with stones and streaks of light: something has died.

Nothing but love dies or is alive.
Religion never dies, it is stone,
the stone and the light are what I believe,
love is the suffering in religion.
In these dead times we are old animals,
and yellow hangs and hangs and never falls.

**171**

Sunrise and sunset dazzle the horses,
up in the mountains a pebble rings,
snowfall relieves the sky and the bald rock
and muffles the dead swirling of the buzzard's wings.

I have never been so high in this valley,
it chills the sun, the faces of hermits
peer downward through the snowspray and lightspray
and cold processions of loose clouds and lights.

Rock-voices magnify like shadows,
and all the music of time is over:
winter as it has never been before,
when the crest is so silent and so sheer.


**172**

And the sea dies. It withers.
And mountains meditate their dying phrase.
The glitter of the frost-reviving sun
streams into a snow-cold, a dying breath.
Heaven is full of unnamed characters:
tragical and slow, padding downwards
apricot into violet. It snows.
A bitter blast of wind from that mouth
tosses heavy lemons on the branches,
enters the little world between houses
which is the leavings of the living God.
The never-ending journeys of old people
between villages in the winter sun.
A snowy rock. A cattle-smell.
And in the summer daisies in the upper pastures.

## 173

Suddenly old and ill
with a Sunday paper on a balcony
I know who I am, I watch a bird,
I am a spark, a trickle, a few stones,
a paper boat of passion out at sea.
We go cold at the core first
and the last few springtimes
flower quiet as ash coming to rest.
It is the possibility of love increasing
that so strangely disturbs the blue immense
and underground is tinkling among boulders.
Sunshine surprises thinness and age,
it was a secret there is this to life.

## 174

The sun of twenty years ago in mist
lemon-coloured in a sweat of weakness:
and a tree of rain in a twist of thunder,
a withered chirping and a tree of rock.
We shall never come through again.
There is something old-fashioned in our eyes.
A wind without words has been blowing.
How many bones make a Parthenon?
The world being a system of seed
a sheet of rock is the end of the dead.
A rain of sun in a forest of stone
will ripen nothing but a wordless wind.

**After Lucian**

Between the dry sun and the dewy moon
runs a fresh amber, a brushed atmosphere
always revolving without dust
between the thorn fire and the marine fleece.
The peacock of heaven is idle for ever,
his eyes swim, and galaxies run down
while he crackles the blue fires on his crest
or loosens the slow springtime of his wings.
The skin of the world is blue and white,
all swirls and shining like an oyster shell,
a bead in the horizon of heaven.
Pace by pace it is sinking further down.
The motion of sunlight is motionless,
it is a coast where the dew hardly dries,
it is a finite and pure element,
and the peacock will drown himself in it.

Maybe we are the last generation
stumbling about in the rough grass.
We came home smelling of freedom.
Mining in prison floors there was a light.
And over many thousands of unburied
the heavy buzzing lifted at moonrise.
Romantic death is over now,
there remains marble-breasted Virtue
with a myrtle-wreath for the fall of dew.
There remains the red sun in the black rain,
unwritten rock, the level, shooting fires.
Dig for the lost root of an early generation,
tall ships harvested silent in flames.
Freedom was an adventurous defence.
Death is a harvest, freedom reaps it down.
An easy smell blowing about a hill
is the beginning of the truth about life.

**177**   (*The Law School Riots, Athens, 1973*)


A kite a blue scratch on a blue sky:
scatter of white snow on a screen of rock,
and the sun pouring away into the sea
greener thinner and colder than honey.
A new stem weeps or sleeps between rocks.
I am dreaming my head is broken rock.
Everything fresh is breathing in one stream:
the breath of rock when we are free in dreams
cracks a bone open, courage is this shock,
scatter of white snow on a screen of rock.


**178**    (*Notes about Kant*)


Think of the eighteenth-century Baltic
and never leaving one provincial town,
playing at cards for money,
hating the imitation of a nightingale.
They felt music was colours on a peach,
preferred a garden to be nearly wild,
used old-fashioned baroque furniture.
The universe of Newton is an iceberg,
the seagulls are mewing every day.
Nothing is free in nature
and my life is a scientific scribble
in link on link on chain on chain of ice.
Philosophy is praxis,
my soul the object of an inner sense.
Nothing not moral can be understood.

## 179    Rivers

*(The Thames, August–November 1973)*


1

The sky dark blue, the sun a butter-pat:
confusion of dark leaf, harvest machines
the shaking and the rattling and the dust.
This small river should grow a new skin.
I wish well to the fish.
I have had this face for forty-two years:
no partridges or hares are in my grain,
then I should grow a sort of river-skin
and glitter and die like a sun-fragment.
Sullen continuation of dark leaf
daubing the moon's road blotching the sun's:
a stronger smell than the dust
a sharper smell than the mist,
living by the confusion of dark leaf.


2

Diving off a road-bridge a young gnat
three seconds in mid-air.
Sunny brick, river so old and green
there might be no upstream,
and is there any pure source to swim in?
I am a tree-head in its own shadow.
Rivers are for upstream.
Long time is for walking beside them.
Or be a bird with crimson at the breast
swoops in what time has eaten running back.
I meditate the sun, his energies,
always walk in the straggle of his rays.

## 3

Come along brain-bone, come and see
this curdled river under sparks of rain
as lucid as a bream ignite himself,
ruffle his bank and run black under it.
Come and climb up into a tree.
Willows with ashes brush together.
The air's electric, heaven is pregnant
but time is slow, the season is slow.
Consider your future O mankind:
only the swans will need no shelter,
they shake their feathers and they die.
I need a shelter. We need a shelter.
The globe is never still.

## 4

Scruffy meadows endless by the railway,
then walking in the wet and shaggy grass
you might plunge your head in the cool sun
and keep on walking. Oh to be still.
Oh sober drunkenness. Yellow light.
The season tilting and the hour tilting.
An animal speaking in a meadow
heavenly mysteries running like rivers
has planted a black shadow on the green.

## 5

Now we are worse than then.
The blighted summer like a throat:
I drink the diseases of London.
You would be silent at such a time,
the chemist has no remedy for love.

A river maintaining a small language,
the monologues of reason,
moss, pebble, autumn flower:
the solitude the river created:
In my head I am walking in it
light as a hare, we are like hares in grass,
and we behave as they do in autumn.


6

It drizzled.
The air is full of leaves and drizzle.
The lamplight is small in the empty road.
Waking at dawn, who I am, where I am.
Once when the lamplighter passed at five
brushing the skin of the wet hedge
the streetlight had long rays like crocodiles.
Much later in the dawn anonymous
the swishing taxis the suburban birds
waking at dawn smelling like a small town.
Oh to be in love in eighteen eighty.
Oh to be at peace in nineteen ten.
I want the future of mankind.
I copy out the music of the people.
Léger painted the bones of the new world.
I write your name.


7

Indoors the images of the Virgin,
doe-eyed mercy, faces from the kitchen.
Moral machines are never in control.
My life has been entangled in a tree,
the dust of books, a cat, the betting-shop,
the stone inside what is alive,
breathing paint-fumes, coughing coal-dust.

It is soon black enough to have courage,
and conversation is black and cold.
There is nowhere except through the leaves,
the rain hangs in the darkening air.


8

A limestone statue in a meadow
cut off by railings is father Thames,
the steady local trickle of his springs
continues like starlight.
Shall be my father and my grandfather.
Trees are the pyramids and spires of light,
they are a coarseness in the mind of God,
he dribbles a streaky-coloured mist
between the greying bodies of the trees.
Is tough enough to talk in English.
The leaves are turning high on every hill.


9

Early winter. It is wet in the field.
There is something discarded about mist.
I like this hush,
ditches of black enamel, motionless dead leaf,
pink in the dawn's cheek,
the ice-axes of light hammer stone.
River-water is moral but obscure.
There is no edge of nature.
There are no contrivances left in the world.
I like to see these robust colours.

**180**

A letter on a dusky wet morning:
to live after us like the smell of rooms,
or like the traditional way robins sing:
so children's manners are candlelight to tombs.
I say a marble head, a snowy rock,
will create space in the surrounding air:
poor masterpiece of light personal shock:
but love never dies out, it is despair.
It lives more than the shape and smell of rooms,
persisting in manners as robins sing,
it is our children, carries light in tombs,
it is the coldest dawn, the clear morning.

**181**     (*Backstreet in Sicily, 1974*)

The sun was smashing open a blue stone,
sweating the waters of the underworld,
the lemon was in fruit in the shadow,
the world is fresh and it will not fall.
A dozen children banging on tin cans
are imitating eighteen forty-eight.
We are re-inventing antiquity,
this beginning will go on many years,
these evils will not outlast our time.

**182**

Wind-bitten architecture the last muse
dying out in the sand.
Further inland hillside after hillside,
a ghostly plumage, a valley of reeds,
and the wild bees are in the rosemary.

He drowned his voice in this green confusion,
growing is slow and easy,
he whittled it away sharpening wood,
like drawing a long line, a casual line:
the engineer's more honourable trade
has ground holes in the rock and in the sky.
There is some blossom on the infirm trees.
He will transform to a red-breasted bird,
brown and blue in the wing learning his note
among trees and the shadows of trees.
The sea is colouring the whole sky.


## 183    A Few Words about Fascism

Wild weeds are not as wet or as cold,
and the gunsmoke of fog on the Danube ice,
the English marshlight and the frozen fell-mist,
the heavy silence that our snow tumbles in
are not so impassable or so bleak
as the spirit creaking in a cage of bones.

The weed lives wild, the morning will clear,
the ice has broken up, the mist also,
the names of the dead are on stone in the sun,
but the spirit is creaking like a bat,
it has sucked at the breast of the mother-bat,
twittering like a wind, blind in the sun.

It has not dropped out of the hand of God,
swollen rivers spitting mouthfuls of stones
are less deep and angry than his thought,
in the inhabitation of spirit
ice is level, the mist is permanent,
it is breathing and howling in that mist.

## 184

I crow and cry that I was a man.
Half the animal voices are human.
I am sunrise, I have become a thing,
and I am foreign without travelling.
I see tapers flicker and trees crash,
there is no heaviness in human ash.
A star flies like a bird, it can expire,
that small tail is a million miles of fire.
Daybreak is just as human as I am.
I crow and cry that I was a man.

## 185

Hung in mid-air, a faint yellow brush
down from sunlight touches the vast ice.
Things of white fur scamper through silence.
Seed of a dandelion carries on the wind.
Who can believe in a future,
the heavy bags of rain to be poured out?
The unnecessary dark colour of fire
dying away with the already dead.
Bloody or unbloody, it is to come
among the wreckage of this element.
Soft-haired, bright-eyed, leather-skinned.

## 186

I take Charlie Chaplin seriously
having had to pay for a dusty seat,
and remember the Gaumont British News.
Pio Nono is dead and no one cares.
There is no fascist architecture in heaven.
Léger is painting the Virgin in heaven.
She waited for him for two thousand years.
In heaven I shall have my passport.
Lorca has written ballads in heaven.
There are no skyscrapers and no sky.
Léger is painting the Virgin in heaven.

## 187

The dark mirror painting strawberry stone,
yellow stone, blue stone, dust.
The sun lives in a ragged garden.
I am an unhappy woman.
There are things I have never understood.
I live with books, it would be cold
combing my hair in the rocky sea.
There is no place my breath would not wither.
I think of an old fellow with white hair,
thump of his heart on dislocated bone,
the mark of his teeth deep in silver,
the mark of the sea's teeth in the rock.
No house is dusty enough,
no garden is ragged enough.

Now with young people dressing in old canvas
and the green tips in the innocent mist
you could be living in ruinous glass-houses
and without running to seed I insist.

With time lazing along and the sky humble,
fresh greenery nuzzling into your hand,
you could live like a water-vole through the summer,
in a ditch you were coming to understand.

Marine light is rebuilding architecture,
before dawn you see animals in the street,
you could be one, but not for the adventure,
you could be hungry and have fur on your feet.

The point of writing is to suffer alteration,
what is worth saying is something common,
writing a long letter may be as fatal
as saying what all history hangs on.

## 189    Officers and Gentlemen

Walking with long legs on the long shadows,
they make the sun look as if it were still,
unstudied time in the declines of time.
They bleed blood as freely as money.
I see them in a lens as they live now.
This world is the fetid and the defeated.
Hunching unwashed in an enormous Rolls,
my fellow driving to the long champagne:
not unfit to command men.
Gods are the measles, a childish disease,
caught for the first time late in life
they corrode manhood. Heroes depend on them,
trailing adolescent legs in the long grass.

**190**   *for Peter and Margaret*

The wooden-shouldered tree is wild and high,
it is a plane-tree lighted inwardly,
it imprisons the sun in a cloth of leaf.
That will escape from this world though,
the tree is deliberate, it is life,
it has a musty smell and a shadow.

Bigger breasted than birds, it is breathing,
hangs with a weightless weight on everything,
having considered the sun from time to time
which vanishes in incense and yellow light:
is as silent as fog, the winter gleam
of a small sun and the birds in their flight.

It is courageous and it is alive,
this tree is nine parts of what I believe:
freedom lies in the inward of nature,
and this tree is green fire in a world of trees,
catches blue air, is neither pure nor impure,
but is alive. It is alive and dies.


**191**


Consider the death of machinery,
there is nothing I honour more than that.
I will invent mechanical mankind,
in singlets under an automatic sun,
severe procedures shall declare times
antlike in the long tuneful desert.
And machines are formidable in sleep,
lie down motionless among oil-smears.
(Eat grass, read a clear-handed writing,
run one race, out-manoeuvre all bones,
thistle-stiff and flower-pink in the cheek.)

Add the three qualities of fine machines,
in freedom, in memory, in fear:
they shall be masters and have music,
and their socialism will be lucid,
their gospel is documentary truth.
What has been well handled has been loved,
what has been well used has been honoured.
They shall live in a mechanical green world.
The noises of machinery at play
will occupy my window at daybreak.
I honour the running down of machines.


**192**


The altering of the season is this.
Memory alters man. I will write down
the blackness and the wetness and wind.
The trees are fine and bushy but still bare,
and the far end of the meadow is misted.
I like the weight and toughness of time,
it will permit a candle to burn down,
it will permit the oak tree to be slow.
Mind and the world consume at the same pace,
and alcoholic sugars in the trees,
the muffled man with the unmuffled throat
and the wet swan consume at the same pace.

## 193

Gums of the bushes among broken rock
are gathered on the soft beard of a goat
grazing a mountain under falls of dew.
The sun is confident, the moon weeps,
and the blush on the sky's face is cold.
The animal wildness of mankind
is spirit, it is gentle quality.
What will not die in him is mountainous,
the clatter of his horns amazes trees,
he washes his soft beard in lake-water.

## 194

The salad-rose and the tea-rose expire
in aromatic shadows on red earth,
and everything is thirsty, it all bends
under the smoke and fire and the sunfumes.
We are not bounded by this world.
I am living in an unwritten bible.
The migrations of horses and of geese
have shifted like the sand-motion of stars,
and the voices of God are planetary.
There is a wild and tossing light that fell
through clear glass on these papers and the walls,
and I saw that the shortest-living weeds
are the most human, and the tree is bare.
The greatness of God is variable.
I think well of the robin and the thrush,
they whistle prophecies like a folk-song,
they are familiar with fearful dark.
Bees take honey high on hot mountains.
The world is always breaking open,
we are among water and light and fire,
and melancholy green, ruinous farms.

## 195

You could never define how they were sad,
fantastical dresses on the light limbs,
an instrument of music, talk of love,
enormous skies, perfectly still trees.
That severe park is a dangerous garden,
lovers cling loosely, the days fall,
a universal dream of private dreams,
why is the sky yellow, the tree blue?
How warm faces light up for one another,
and as there was no role for them to play
they wandered away into the mown grass.

## 196

This season has been carried away dead.
It is black before tea-time;
dramatic curtains cover the afternoon,
we are shut up in the madhouse of a dream,
like a twig where the first and the last bird cried.

All the thoughts of tragedy are lifelike,
the belly spouts rhetorical fire,
what one bird cried before
shall be enacted now, yet not appear
more than a waterdrop when the trees break.

They have gathered in curious energies,
they will let it all loose
in one storm-burst, a travesty of peace.
The final state of nature is repose.
A storm is a black swan smelling of spice.

## 197

When the great actor with the dying eyes
creates an unimprinted empty sea,
and the whole of the sea is quiet,
the footbeat of that quiet is despair
and the seafoam is love in his language,
it is honourable in his language.

When the small herdboys cry out at dusk
and heads of cattle toss in their long stream,
daylight and dust dissolve,
there is something final about darkness,
mountains are honourable by starlight,
and villages of men are honourable.

## 198

In the green glow under trees
they drowse hand in hand,

with a whisper of harshness
they will divide a star cold as fruit,

and on the pavement spotting with rain
they lose themselves in long conversation.

In a dusk noisy with birds
they descend from mountains,

and the rainclouds and the blossoming trees
inspire them to consider geometry.

Through lazy summer
they carry frost under their tongues.

# Index of Titles and First Lines

(Titles are in bold type. The numbers refer to pages.)